WITHDRAWN

D0041593

Praise For

"Almost every day we hear one more story about a species facing extinction, a habitat destroyed. And indeed, planet earth has never been so threatened by human actions. This is why *Wild Lives* is so desperately important. The people in this book are united by their belief that it is not too late to turn things around. You will be inspired by their stories. You will realize that there is hope for the future if we join the fight, if each of us does our bit."

—Jane Goodall, PhD, DBE, and UN Messenger of Peace,
founder of the Jane Goodall Institute

"Fighting for sanctuary and safety for those most precious to them, these wildlife heroes are up against extraordinary odds, yet their courage and sacrifice remains undaunted. From melting icecaps to humid jungles, these people have dedicated their lives to helping those who can never say thank you. Robinson and Chodosh weave masterful narratives around these people, in stories that are even more astounding because they are true. *Wild Lives* brings into clear focus the incredible animals with whom we share the world. Be careful, it will make you want to quit your job and join the fight to save them."

—Vanessa Woods, *New York Times* bestselling
author of *Bonobo Handshake*

"The twenty lives documented in this compelling book are truly remarkable in their diversity and commitment to conservation of species and habitats. I loved reading about each and every one of them, the different problems they encounter protecting animals and their bold and insightful solutions—a wonderful read."

—Jane Alexander, actress; author
of *Wild Things, Wild Places*

"*Wild Lives* is a most important contribution to the broad field of conservation biology. The biographical stories of twenty major contributors who constitute a who's who of scientists who have worked tirelessly to save our planet—it's magnificent and awe-inspiring fauna and flora—are and inspirational pieces. We are living in an epoch called the Anthropocene, often called "the age of humanity." In reality, it is "the rage of inhumanity." This book should be on the shelf of everyone who cares about our wondrous and fragile planet, from youngsters to seniors in all parts of the world, who want to see our nonhuman animals and plants thrive and survive despite so much that is being done that is contributing to its rapid demise. *Wild Lives* should be required reading for all humans, and adults should read it to youngsters, because they are ambassadors for the future. Animals and their homes need all the help they can get, and the people whose moving stories and accomplishments are covered in this book readily serve as inspirational role models for the future."

—Marc Bekoff, editor of *Ignoring Nature No More: The Case for Compassionate Conservation* and author of *The Animal's Agenda: Freedom, Compassion, and Coexistence in the Human Age*

"*Wild Lives* is a salute to the people on the front lines of conservation. Having worked with animals myself, specifically elephants, many people have inspired me, but mostly it was the elephants that inspired me. Through narratives based on personal interviews with twenty of the world's conservation champions, readers will get an insider's view to what it takes to save some of the planet's greatest species."

—Dr. Iain Douglas-Hamilton, co-author of *Among the Elephants* and *Battle for the Elephants*

"Some people say we live in a time when there are no more environmental heroes. Fortunately for us, *Wild Lives* proves them wrong. The stories in this uplifting book will inspire you to make a difference. They show that heroes for the planet can be found everywhere, among both young and old. You, too, can be a hero!"

—Todd Wilkinson, author and environmental journalist

"Great conservationists are the warriors that step up to defend our planet. Man has declared an insidious war on the earth. Each person in *Wild Lives*, many of whom I can call friends, is a hero who heard the whisper of this war before it became a roar; they saw the signs before they became front-page news; they heeded a call that was as yet unspoken. Their work is on the unrelenting front line of ecological destruction. They have dedicated their lives to protecting our landscapes and all the species we share them with. Mere thanks and admiration fall short. This book inspires us to follow where they lead, and to join them in striving to love and protect our earth-home."

—Thomas D. Mangelsen, legendary nature photographer

Wild Lives

Leading Conservationists on the Animals and the Planet They Love

LORI ROBINSON

AND JANIE CHODOSH

Skyhorse Publishing

Copyright © 2017 by Lori Robinson and Janie Chodosh

All rights reserved. No part of this book may be reproduced in any manner without the express written consent of the publisher, except in the case of brief excerpts in critical reviews or articles. All inquiries should be addressed to Skyhorse Publishing, 307 West 36th Street, 11th Floor, New York, NY 10018.

Skyhorse Publishing books may be purchased in bulk at special discounts for sales promotion, corporate gifts, fund-raising, or educational purposes. Special editions can also be created to specifications. For details, contact the Special Sales Department, Skyhorse Publishing, 307 West 36th Street, 11th Floor, New York, NY 10018 or info@skyhorsepublishing.com.

Skyhorse® and Skyhorse Publishing® are registered trademarks of Skyhorse Publishing, Inc.®, a Delaware corporation.

Visit our website at www.skyhorsepublishing.com.

10 9 8 7 6 5 4 3 2 1

Library of Congress Cataloging-in-Publication Data is available on file.

Cover design by Tom Lau
Cover photo credits: Top Left: Dee Boersma; Top Right: Gabriel Vianna; Center: Eli Walker/Cheetah Conservation; Bottom Right: David White/IFAW; Bottom Left: Kelly Landen, Elephants Without Borders.

Print ISBN: 978-1-5107-1364-2
Ebook ISBN: 978-1-5107-1365-9

Printed in the United States of America

This book is for all the wild ones with whom we share our planet
and to all those dedicated to saving them.

Contents

Foreword

by Carl Safina

It's a terrible time for nature. Plants and animals are going extinct because of humans. And never mind extinction. Even for species who aren't endangered, we often hear it remarked that species so-and-so "is still common." The key word is "still." We all know what that implies; it implies that the trend is down. Not just big beings like apes and elephants, but birds and bugs and pretty much everything.

Virtually every non-human being is at its lowest population level since we strolled in. You can intuit this immediately by looking at the proxy for species—their habitats. All kinds of habitats—forests, grasslands, freshwaters, coral reefs, the ocean—are at all-time lows of quality and size. If we're driving down *everything*, it means something rather startling. It means that at this point in history, humans are not compatible with Life on Earth.

Now, I'm not against humans. After all, I am one. And some of my best friends are people. So I have a lot invested in humanity. But at this stage we've got to admit that we're just too much of a good thing. What's the plan? There are more than twice as many people on our planet now as when I was born. Isn't that staggering? Many people more expert than I say that the human population will continue increasing until there's at least a third more of us than there are now. And for so many who are dismally poor, who lack basic dignity and a decent shot at life, the situation looks even bleaker than numbers alone can tell. How can we take care of anything while we can barely take care of ourselves? Often it seems we can't.

Every day there is more carbon dioxide in the air. Every day the ocean is just a bit more acidic. Every day more plastic washes down rivers into the sea, where it will last basically forever. To seabirds, plastic smells like food. Turtles and whales, too, eat the bite-sized pieces that they cannot digest. Frogs and bats are dying of fungus. Forests are crashing. Poachers are out killing day and night.

Wow.

Who can bear all this? Isn't it just too depressing? It would take a superhero to know about this and not get overwhelmed, and still try to do something about it. In fact, it would take an army of such people. They would have to have superhuman powers, but they'd also need feel everything that humans like you and me can feel. And they'd have to keep on going in spite of it all, able to absorb bad news like champion fighters and yet get over and on with it in superhuman ways. They'd have to feel inspired and empowered. They'd get crushed and pop up again, ready to go at it. And they'd have to have special powers to inspire and empower any human who saw them.

Yes, such superhuman superheroes would be just about the only hope for what lives in the world, the only hope for Earth's life-support systems like air and land and waters, the only hope for all the plants and animals. The *only* hope!

Now here's the thing—I'm going to tell you a little secret. There are no such superhuman superheroes. But luckily for all of us, there are *human* superheroes. More than you know. More than you might think. More than you'd guess. And when a species *doesn't* go extinct, when birds *still* migrate, where giraffes *still* run and lions *still* rule and elephants continue trumpeting to the sky—it's because of them. It's because of them that many whales once near extinction are now common again in some parts of the ocean, and falcons are back and eagles soar in greater numbers and wolves again roam where they were missing for a hundred years. Only a super human could do that. And they have. That's what they do, and they're doing it at this very moment.

So get ready. Turn the page. You're going to meet them now.

Introduction

Conservation. It may be one of the most depressing fields to work in right now. The hurdles to overcome are enormous, the stakes higher than any time in human history. As Thomas Lovejoy explains in the first chapter: "One species per one thousand years was the extinction rate in recent millions of years. Today the rate is at least one thousand times that, if not ten thousand times that. It is the only time a mass extinction has been caused by a single species. Humans." So why would anyone choose a career trying to protect wildlife and wild places? Yet the conservationists in *Wild Lives* have done just that, and they still remain hopeful.

🐾

We both earned degrees in environmental science, Janie a master's from University of Montana and Lori a bachelor's from University of California Santa Cruz. Janie then became an environmental educator first in Yosemite National Park and eventually in New Mexico, and Lori worked for wildlife NGOs, including The Jane Goodall Institute, and started SavingWild.com. For years we have followed the careers of many of the conservationists in *Wild Lives,* but it wasn't until we met each other for the first time in early summer 2015—Lori with an idea and interviews with some of the conservationists, and Janie fresh from the publication of her first novel—that we decided we needed to do this book together.

Wild Lives is a compilation of the personal stories of twenty conservationists across the globe. We interviewed each person, asking them: How did you start your career? Why did you choose your particular species? What is a day in your life like? What are the scariest, most challenging, and most rewarding parts of your work? How do you stay inspired? And what have you learned that you can pass on to the next generation of conservationists?

Some of the people in *Wild Lives* have been thrown in jail and thrown out of countries, are hated by hunters and hunted by rebels. They work in some of the remotest areas in the world, in all kinds of weather. They have used sea ice for a pillow, been charged by elephants, bitten by snakes, and chased by rhino. "I can't even recall how many times I've had malaria or nearly died," Dereck Joubert says. All of them are breaking boundaries, trying new ways of doing things, and challenging the status quo, such as Yossi Leshem, using birds to bring peace to the Middle East; Farwiza Farhan, speaking out against corporations to save the Leuser Ecosystem; and Megan Parker, training dogs to stop poachers.

Wild Lives is devoted to the notion that conservation can, does, and will work. This book is for everyone who has a passion for saving wildlife and wild places. Thomas Lovejoy believes if something is not gone, it can still be saved. We are facing a dark time, but as Mike Chase reminds us, like the twenty people in *Wild Lives*, we must all be stubborn optimists; otherwise we all lose.

Editor's Note: All the conservationists interviewed in *Wild Lives* approved their stories before the book went to press.

CHAPTER 1

• • •

Thomas Lovejoy, PhD: The Man Who Coined "Biological Diversity"

"If something's not gone, it can still be saved."

—Thomas Lovejoy

Credit: Thomas Lovejoy

Thomas Lovejoy.

IN 1965, WHEN THOMAS LOVEJOY first traveled to the Brazilian Amazon with his former advisor at Yale University and the head of vertebrate zoology at the Smithsonian Institution, he was struck by what he *didn't* see. The writings of the great early naturalists and explorers of the Amazon—including Henry Walter Bates, Alexander von Humboldt, Richard Spruce, and Alfred Russell Wallace—had led him to expect a colorful landscape, teeming with butterflies, monkeys, and birds. Instead, the forest was a wall of green. Besides ants, there seemed to be no animals in sight.

Lovejoy began to learn what was living under the canopy, in the understory and on the forest floor, and in the tangles of vines and enormous towering trees, by netting and banding birds. Once he had them in hand and began observing, he learned to see by learning to hear. "After a while you learn to listen and then to figure out where the sound is coming from and what is making the sound. And then you begin to notice detail." With more than 1,500 species of birds in the Amazon, nearly a third of which are endemic—meaning that they are species found nowhere else—learning to identify them takes time. Lovejoy has given the Amazon that time. He has returned to Brazil for countless visits since that trip in 1965. "I go to the Amazon with such frequency that I have given up explaining. I just say I am always on my way to the Amazon."

Although the Amazon is where Lovejoy conducts much of his field research (including the Biological Dynamics of Forest Fragmentation Project, a nearly forty-year ecological experiment looking at the effects of habitat fragmentation and seeking to define the minimum size for national parks and biological reserves as well as management strategies for small areas), he also just likes to go to a place of "perpetual biological surprise, where I can listen to the howler monkeys and other jungle noises from my hammock."

🐾

Lovejoy's passion for nature began as a small child. Born in 1941, he grew up in Manhattan, but spent most summers outside of the city at the New Jersey shore, in New Hampshire, and on Fire Island, where he could go outside and explore nature. When he was four years old he got to spend a year on the eastern shore of Maryland with one of his father's sisters. Lovejoy recalls, "There's a famous family story about when I interrupted my uncle and father and said, 'Can we talk about something interesting like snakes and skunks?'" The handwriting was on the wall by that point, but what really sparked Lovejoy's interest in biology was a teacher. "As an only child, my father thought I should get out from under foot and be on my own," says Lovejoy, so at age thirteen, he started looking for boarding schools. The one that caught his interest was the Millbrook School with its zoo. "I was really taken by the zoo because I already loved animals," says Lovejoy. "I announced that was where I wanted to go. Luckily, I was able to get in."

Ironically, Lovejoy wasn't interested in pursuing classes in science and thought he would take biology his first year and "get it over with." Frank Trevor, his biology teacher and the man behind the Millbrook zoo, changed all that. "Three weeks into that class with an incredible biology teacher, he flipped my switch. His style of teaching was contagious enthusiasm," says Lovejoy. "He taught biology in such a way that before the age of fifteen I understood the outline of life on earth. I've never been able to get enough of it ever since. That was pretty exciting."

This experience was so exciting that from high school Lovejoy went on to earn both a bachelor's and a PhD in biology from Yale. His 1971 PhD thesis introduced the technique of bird banding to Brazil and was the first major long-term study of birds in the Amazon. Though Lovejoy's work in Brazil has been key in raising international awareness about the issue of tropical deforestation, in 2016, fifty-one years after his first visit to the Amazon, the world's largest forest is still being unsustainably cut down for soy plantations, timber, and cattle, among other things. Lovejoy, however, is optimistic, and maintains hope for one of the most important ecosystems on earth:

> In the Amazon twenty-five years ago, if somebody suggested that a quarter of it would be under some form of protection, they would've carted you off to some sort of mental institution. And in fact, over 50 percent is under protection today. And while I can tell you that's not enough to protect the hydrologic cycle (the Amazon creates half of its own rainfall, meaning that transpiration from trees creates clouds, which in turn produces rain—without enough trees, that cycle is interrupted), it's extraordinary.

Besides his work in the Amazon, Lovejoy has had a prestigious career in academia, conservation, and policy. He has, among other things, served as the director of conservation at the World Wildlife Fund, the assistant secretary for environmental and external affairs at the Smithsonian Institution, and the chief biodiversity advisor to the president of the World Bank, as well as the lead specialist for Latin America and the Caribbean. He has served on science and environmental councils under Presidents Reagan, H. W. Bush, and Clinton. He founded the series *Nature* for public television, has been awarded numerous international conservation prizes (including the esteemed Tyler Prize for Environmental Achievement in 2001 and the Blue Planet Prize in 2012), and is now senior fellow at the United Nations Foundation in Washington, DC, and professor in the Department of Environmental Science and Policy at George Mason University.

Despite all these accomplishments, Thomas Lovejoy is perhaps best known as the man who coined the phrase "biological diversity" (the totality of diversity from the genetic level, through organisms, to ecosystems, and landscapes), a phrase that is now such a part of the conservation lexicon it is hard to imagine a time when it wasn't in existence. Although he is modest and careful to credit other legendary conservationists with initial use of the term, the scientific community generally agrees that Lovejoy was first. "In the late 1970s there were a bunch of people concerned about developing the science for conservation and concerned about the state of nature," he explains. "And we were concerned about biological diversity, but we didn't have a term for it. There were three people who started using it in 1980: Ed Wilson, myself, and Elliot Norse. None of us were thinking who was first and that we were doing something new. It was just so natural. It was only later that Elliot went back and looked in the printed record and determined I was first—first by a short bit of time."

In discussing the importance of biological diversity, Lovejoy says, "Each species presents a set of solutions—pretested by evolution—to a particular set of biological problems. All of them have the potential to make substantial contributions to a sustainable future." It is difficult to imagine the degree to which the tree of life can provide solutions when, as Lovejoy says, "We can't even get within a factor of ten of the number of species on the planet. If you include microorganisms, the number is off the charts." Here is an educated guess: according to the Center for Biological Diversity, current estimates of global species diversity is somewhere between thirteen and fourteen million, the majority of them belonging to the arthropod family (insects, spiders, centipedes, shrimp, and crayfish). Of this vast number, a third is believed to be at risk of extinction, and only about 1.5 million have been described. Biological diversity, according to Lovejoy, "is a vast library for the life sciences, which is drawn upon to improve critical biologically based enterprises like agriculture and medicine." In fact, almost half of the pharmaceuticals used in the United States today are made using natural compounds. Many of these compounds cannot be manufactured in a laboratory.

While many people talk about protecting biological diversity and the environment for their children and grandchildren, Lovejoy, who has three grown daughters, talks about ecosystem protection on a much more expansive scale. According to him, maintaining biological diversity means that the species list one hundred or five hundred years from now should be comparable to what it is today. With the growth in global population and the pressure on land and sea intensifying, however, extinction rates have reached unprecedented levels.

Conservation scientists all agree that we are in the midst of the sixth mass extinction event. "One species per one thousand years was the extinction rate in recent millions of years," explains Lovejoy. "Today the rate is at least one thousand times that, if not ten thousand times that. It is the only time a mass extinction has been caused by a single species. Humans." With characteristic optimism, Lovejoy believes we are still in the early stages of this extinction event, and it is not too late to "rise above our self-centered ways." Ultimately, it is a change in attitude toward nature that Lovejoy sees as the most important factor in conservation. He remarks:

> As powerful and imperative as I believe the practical arguments for conservation are, a change in perception and value about our place in nature could achieve vastly more. We have to flip our model from one in which nature exists in little isolated patches in human dominated landscapes to one in which human aspiration is embedded in nature. When the public understands that the planet works as a linked biological and physical system and that ecosystem restoration can help avoid some climate change, then they will understand they are part of the living planet and should value and care for it.

To truly recognize that "human aspiration" is tied to ecosystem function, we must see the true value of these services, which, Lovejoy asserts, "are treated as free and therefore mostly left out of decision-making until finally a tipping point is reached and the service fails." In order to avoid these tipping points, we must think of the entire planet as one continuous living system, and of course we must think about the Amazon. What happens in the Amazon affects all of us. "You can't heal the planet without taking care of the tropical rainforest," says Lovejoy. For example, without the Amazon, the greenhouse effect would be far greater—not to mention that the Amazon influences ocean currents and weather patterns across the globe. And then there's the oxygen that all those trees produce.

Now in his mid-seventies, Lovejoy says, "It's time to think big. My view is that every morning I wake up and look at it as a fresh challenge. And if something's not gone, that means it can still be saved. I don't think there's any option but to be optimistic about being able to make a difference. What value is there in sitting around wringing your hands and moaning and groaning?" Lovejoy is far from sitting around. In 2016, he is working on a third book on biodiversity and climate change with Lee Hannah, and after that he has at least two more books he wants to write. Besides writing, he is pushing hard to "re-green the emerald planet." With the goal of re-greening in mind, he wants to restore ecosystems on a planetary scale. "Because that's not only good for biodiversity, it also pulls a lot of carbon dioxide out of the atmosphere before it creates climate change," he says. "At this stage of my career I'm trying to affect things on a really large scale, which means that I try and facilitate other groups and other people to engage in these things, rather than getting sidetracked in pursuing just one."

Saving wild places, maintaining biological diversity, and ensuring the future of our planet is something that Lovejoy sees as everyone's responsibility. "Each of us can contribute in different ways—whether it's as a poet or a field biologist," he says. "Where precisely you start is less important than just starting and finding good mentors. Just make sure you know enough science, or have access to it, so that what you do is scientifically sound. Just show you care, are eager to help and to learn. Find out what your local conservation organization is doing. Know what your elected officials are doing. Speak up."

Speaking up and changing our relationship with nature starts at home. "Create habitat. Plant milkweed for the monarchs," says Lovejoy. Backyard habitats can provide some of the connectivity, the re-wilding, and the change to human dominated landscapes, which re-greening the emerald planet requires. But, as Lovejoy has said, it is ultimately a change in attitude, one in which we see ourselves as part of nature as opposed to separate from, that matters most. One way Lovejoy believes people can establish this connection is simple: "Get outside and experience nature, hear it and feel it," he says.

As a pioneer in the field of conservation, Lovejoy believes that biological diversity is the single measure of how humanity is affecting the environment. Our future depends on how well we can provide for the future of all other forms of life.

For more information on Thomas Lovejoy and the concept of biological diversity, please visit www.centerforbiodiversityandsustainability. weebly.com and www.amazonbiodiversitycenter.org.

• • •

CHAPTER 2

Beverly and Dereck Joubert: Ambassadors for African Wildlife and Wilderness

"Who would think a wild leopard could teach you so much about love, compassion, and empathy?"

—Beverly Joubert

Credit: Wildlife Films

Dereck and Beverly Joubert.

AS THICK AFTERNOON CLOUDS BUILD above Botswana's Okavango Delta, a three-month-old leopard senses the impending storm and takes cover in a cluster of bushes. Alone and away from her mother, the cub silently waits while the sky cracks open and heavy rain begins to fall. Suddenly, a bolt of lightning hits a tree fewer than twenty paces from where she crouches. The sound is deafening, and the electrical discharge is strong enough to knock the leaves from the branches.

A few yards from the cub, Beverly and Dereck Joubert, celebrated *National Geographic* filmmakers and explorers-in-residence, wait in their open-sided jeep to see if she will emerge. They're hoping to film the young leopard, to document her story, and in doing so, to tell the greater story of her species.

"What happened next," says Beverly, "changed our lives."

🐾

When Beverly was a young girl growing up in Johannesburg, South Africa, her parents introduced her to wildlife. "My parents loved animals, both domestic and wild, and so I was brought up enjoying family safaris," she says. "The trips were different than the way Dereck and I live now. We used to travel in air-conditioned cars with all the windows closed at any animal sightings, as that was the law in the parks. In many ways I couldn't connect with nature, but I always wanted to." At a very young age, Beverly told her parents that she would be different than they were. "I wanted to explore, travel, and discover Africa. I hoped my parents would understand and wouldn't be disappointed." As she got older, Beverly's desire to explore became stronger, as did her longing to help the animals she loved. "As a teenager I was troubled by humanity and what people were doing to each other and to other creatures, and I wanted that to change."

Dereck's introduction to wildlife also occurred at a young age; specifically, it happened in an art studio where, as a child, he watched his older brother—who spent months away from home on adventures in the bush—paint cheetahs, lions, and elephants. "The images emerged magically as he worked his brushes across the large canvas, and I fell in love with the wild, the mystery, and the allure of the large, iconic African animals," says Dereck. "I knew exploration would be my destiny. It was in my DNA from the time I was five." In addition to learning about wildlife through his brother, Dereck learned about art. "I fell in love with the storytelling that is implied in great works of art, be they in oil, bronze, or celluloid. I eventually picked up a camera."

When Beverly and Dereck met at Florida Park High School in Johannesburg, they became sweethearts, and in their early twenties, after Beverly went to college and Dereck went to university, they traveled across eastern and southern Africa together. In 1981, the couple visited the Okavango Delta, where they fell in love with the wildness of the place. "This is when it all came together for us," says Beverly. "It was thrilling and we were driven with passion to discover the unknown." Dereck adds, "Going to Botswana for the first time was like coming home for me. It's a place where you can go and get lost and nobody would care or come looking for you."

Once in Botswana, the Jouberts worked for the Chobe Lion Research Institute (CLRI), which was established to research the nocturnal hunting behavior of lions, about which nothing was known. Dereck's job was doing research and photography, largely to collect visual examples of this mysterious aspect of lions' lives. It was here that he uncovered a movie camera and took it out to collect moving images. That day, while Dereck was shooting footage of a hippo struggling in a drying-up river, he discovered he had an aptitude for filmmaking. Beverly's talent was in stills and sound recording, and the two became a team. In 1985 they officially founded their company, Wildlife Films. Since then, the Jouberts have produced more than thirty documentaries on species from elephants to leopards to rhinos to lions, all of which have a strong conservation message at their core.

After that intense lightning strike, the Jouberts worried that the leopard cub would associate them with the noise and come to fear their presence. "Instead she ran to us and sat with her back against our vehicle close to Dereck's legs, as we do not have doors," they recall. "She was shaking from the hit and getting drenched, but she would not leave our side." On that day, Beverly and Dereck named the leopard cub "Legadema," meaning "Light of the Sky" in the Tswana language—the Bantu tongue spoken in Botswana. By the time Legadema was five months old, she had become part of the Jouberts' lives. Beverly explains:

> We have a policy never to touch an animal and influence it
> or to interfere, intervene, or take sides when nature is taking its course, but what was happening to us was unique;

Legadema was breaking all of those rules. She would greet us every day we found her with a gentle tap on my foot with her paw and would then go under the vehicle and do something similar to Dereck on his side. Often she would gently take Dereck's foot into her mouth, playfully. Each moment observing her changed our lives, and she allowed us into her world—it was intimate and profound. We both knew we had a huge responsibility to help protect big cats. We felt we had to be their ambassadors after having so many special experiences with them.

Dereck and Beverly spent the next five years following and filming Legadema and her mother for what became their famous *National Geographic* documentary, *Eye of the Leopard* (2006), a film that has been seen by tens of millions of people around the world.

From then on, the Jouberts believed that if they kept telling the stories of the animals they filmed in an intimate and personal manner, then those animals would have a better chance for survival. Beverly says, "We look for ways to get our audience to connect with a species through a particular character. By turning their hearts to one powerful animal, it can change the perception of one whole species and the urgency of the situation. We must touch people's hearts as well as their minds." On this statement, Dereck elaborates, "We use filmmaking to influence people against destroying nature. Without conservation, nature fails; without nature, our souls wither, ecosystems fail, culture disappears, and it takes with it our integrity, our self-worth, our common drive to strive for better. If we lose this battle, we don't just lose animals, we lose our souls." It was their time with Legadema that truly turned the Jouberts into "ambassadors," advocates for the voiceless.

It was not just *Eye of the Leopard* that fueled their mission and what Beverly calls their "obsession" to be wildlife ambassadors. Their 2010 film, *Living with Big Cats*, also furthered this pursuit and resulted in the birth of the Big Cats Initiative (BCI) in 2009, which she and Dereck cofounded with *National Geographic*. With eighty grants provided in twenty-seven countries, the mission of BCI is "to halt the decline of big cats across the globe with on-the-ground conservation projects, education, economic incentive efforts, and a public awareness campaign."

The Jouberts have no problem living without things most people call necessities, such as electricity and running water. Working eighteen-hour days in intense heat with major storms is just a part of what they do. Getting sick, charged by elephants and lions, bitten by poisonous snakes and scorpions, crashing small planes—it's all part of the territory. "I can't even recall how many times I've had malaria or nearly died," Dereck says. "I do know I've been bitten by three snakes considered deadly, been attacked by elephants four times, buffalo twice, have had twenty scorpion stings, and crashed three planes. It seems to be working out for us so far, though." They are completely exposed to the elements, and being that they work in remote areas, a quick exit is not an option. "All this makes our lives harder, but without experiencing the hardships we couldn't truly experience the wilderness or become emotionally moved by it," says Beverly. "By stripping everything away, it's easier to find this connection. Our films are filled with the emotions that we feel."

But would they change their lives for a more comfortable existence? No way.

"Obviously when we're in the wilderness we don't have all the luxuries the Western world has become dependent on," Beverly says. "However, we often ask ourselves: Do we really need them? They're wonderful when they're around and make life much easier, but when we're in the field, they become unimportant, especially when we've gotten used to living without them."

Unimportant things, as defined by the Jouberts, are basics such as running hot and cold water, fresh food—which would require refrigeration—and communication devices. Of course, without reliable communication, their social lives are affected. They lose contact with close friends and families, as they are completely on their own for months at a time when they make a film.

There are also other more personal sacrifices to the life they have chosen:

> We made a decision that we'd be more effective in our work if we didn't have children. Each film we've made has been filled with the passion we'd have given to a family, had we

created one. It would've been impossible to try to create both. Over time we've found that we've taken on surrogate relationships with animals, even though they're wild creatures and completely untamed. By living with them daily, they've become our family and we speak out for them, as one would do for their own bloodline. This has helped us look at the larger picture and no matter what we'd given up, it's allowed us to focus our time, energy, and passion on world issues, and that's a worthwhile sacrifice.

The Jouberts might not have their own children, but their films and books have reached millions of children around the world. Each day they receive dozens of letters and drawings from young people whose lives they have touched.

In the early eighties, when Beverly and Dereck first began filming wildlife, they got an up-close look at the atrocities against nature happening throughout Africa. "The bush meat trade was increasing as poverty increased, and safari hunting continued to take out the best and the largest male lions and leopards, thus removing the genes of the best specimens and ever weakening the whole species," says Beverly. This is when the couple first realized that they were more than filmmakers. Their role, first and foremost, was to be conservationists. They started to dialogue with governments, local villages, and the local community about solutions. They explain:

> Now isn't the time to be complacent. We're losing animals at an alarming rate. The facts are disturbing, yet we can't hide from them. Around five lions a day are murdered for their bones for the Asian market or for a trophy or in retaliation killings by villages and communities. One rhino every 6.3 hours is killed. They're now worth more dead than alive, and it's all for a bogus cure or status symbol. Four elephants an hour are killed for their ivory throughout Africa. It's not surprising that over a fifty-year period we've lost between 90 and 95 percent of Africa's large predators. This onslaught can't continue, as we're simply wiping them out. Large predators have gone extinct in twenty-six African countries already.

These facts and figures are overwhelming and hard to stomach for anyone with a love of wildlife, but for the Jouberts, the numbers are not just data points. The numbers are personal. One of those dead lions could have been a part of their surrogate family—one whose story Beverly and Dereck were telling.

But the Jouberts do not quit. They will not stop speaking up for Africa's animals. There is urgency in their work, knowing that time is running out for many species. That urgency is what keeps them going. "Wildlife and nature are our greatest natural treasures, priceless and irreplaceable," they say. "We live in a connected world, and with a collective heart and mind we can, and must, end this destruction. While there is hope, we will fight for them."

Despite the fight, the disheartening numbers, and the sacrifices, both are optimists at heart. "If I was not," Beverly says, "I couldn't continue." More than optimism, what keeps Beverly going is a deep wisdom about the nature of her work and the nature of sacrifice in general. "If we focus only on the sacrifices we've made, then life will certainly become unpleasant and unrewarding. So there's another way of looking at sacrifices—they've turned us into who we are today: advocates and ambassadors for the African wilderness and its wildlife, particularly big cats, as by protecting them and their habitat, we protect every other animal. Every sacrifice can be seen as a gain. It's just about always seeing the positive in whatever life hands you and doing the best you can with it to achieve all that you can be, for yourself and the world around you."

As for his optimism, Dereck uses filmmaking as an analogy. "See life as if it's perfectly framed. Look for the good light and the best composition and framing because it will make you view life in a more perfect way, and then work on making that true."

The advice the Jouberts offer to anyone interested in becoming a wildlife advocate is not about following any one path; it is not about the kind of camera one should hold, the film school one should attend, or the degree one should earn. It is simply about the traits one needs to possess. "Curiosity, compassion, and a sense of adventure are all important qualities," they say. "One must have compassion for all life forms, a yearning to understand the unknown, and to discover and explore. Integrity in this is gold, something we hang onto every single day. Compromising values when it comes to life, or in particular, to conservation, leads to a steady corruption of everything around you."

Being tenacious is another characteristic that helps the Jouberts, the drive to never give up, no matter what it takes. "As huge as some of these issues are, we're not afraid to take them on. As the issues get bigger, so do our ideas, projects, and solutions." They also speak of the importance of ethics. "This may not be an innate quality, but you do have to be the type of person who has a set of ethics and sticks to them, even when times get tough. If you want to set an example and inspire others to do the same, you must know what you stand for and live and breathe it."

Besides these qualities, the Jouberts offer this to aspiring wildlife advocates: "Don't give up in the face of adversity—sometimes you need a second skin, as you're always going to face people who are ethically corrupt and will try to undermine your work. You must stand firm in your beliefs and confront the issues, even if you're the only one standing. Conservation can sometimes be a slow, emotional process, and you'll sometimes take one step forward and many steps back, but eventually we will hopefully succeed."

The Jouberts understand this advice from firsthand knowledge, as demonstrated by a story Beverly recounts about one of the most magnificent bull elephants in Kenya that she and Dereck got to know and film. After six years of following the animal, poachers speared him. His death was long and slow. "It's at times like these that you must take emotional trauma and funnel it into positive action to find solutions to prevent it from happening again."

With this resolve, Beverly and Dereck have started many powerful and innovative conservation initiatives. One such enterprise is the turning of ex-hunting land into nature reserves, and they have already had some great successes. In an eight-year period, starting in 2006, they were able to significantly increase the wildlife in the Selinda Game Reserve, a wildlife sanctuary in northern Botswana where the Selinda Spillway links the Okavango Delta with the Linyanti and Kwando wetlands and rivers.

To push their conservation outreach even further, they started Great Plains Conservation (2006), of which Dereck is CEO. The goal of this company is to secure African landscapes at a large enough scale to protect resident and seasonal wildlife populations. Today that makes up about 1.1 million acres of reclaimed or protected land in Botswana, Zimbabwe, and Kenya. Together with their charitable arm of the company, Great Plains

Foundation, they have started various initiatives to save Africa's wildlife and to "uplift, educate, and care for the surrounding communities."
Of the many community and conservation-based initiatives they have
launched with Great Plains Conservation, their latest enterprise, in partnership with the Botswana-based ecotourism company called & Beyond,
is Rhinos Without Borders.

With rhinos being poached faster than they can breed, the Jouberts
are worried about the future of these animals and want to stop this
trend. "If we stand by and watch the annual count of poached rhinos
rise, we predict there will be no free-roaming rhinos left in Africa within
five years," says Dereck. "The story of rhinos is the story of all wildlife
either now or in the near future unless we act now."

The goal of Rhinos Without Borders is to translocate one hundred rhinos from South Africa to the comparative safety of neighboring Botswana with its low human population density (one-twentieth of
that of South Africa) and large wildlife reserves. As of November 2015,
they had already moved twenty-six rhinos out of a high-risk poaching
environment and secured funding to move another thirty. "Twenty-six
down, budget for thirty more, forty-four to go to reach our target of one
hundred," says Dereck. The Jouberts hope that this protected population
will form a breeding nucleus and help to save a species rapidly heading
for extinction. With this goal in mind, it was a moment to celebrate
when in summer 2016 at least one of the rhinos they moved had a baby.

As the Jouberts see it, it isn't just rhinos and other iconic species
that are threatened. It's the economy of many African nations. "Ecotourism is an enormous industry in East and South Africa, about 80 billion
US dollars a year," explains Dereck. "Much of the money comes from
wildlife safaris to see 'the Big Five'—lions, leopards, rhinos, elephants,
and buffalo. If these species disappear, it will likely set off a chain re-
action in which tourism revenue declines, poverty rises, and poaching
increases."

Besides making films and starting conservation organizations, in
their close to four decades of work, passion, dedication, and near-death
experiences, the Jouberts have written ten books, six scientific papers,
and dozens of articles for *National Geographic*. They have won numerous awards for their films, including eight Emmys and a prestigious
Peabody (started in 1941 to recognize excellence and importance in storytelling using electronic media), to name a few. In 2011, the president

of Botswana honored them for their work within the country with the Presidential Order of Meritorious Service. And in their spare time away from the bush, they have appeared on numerous television shows, including *The Ellen DeGeneres Show*, *The NBC Today Show*, and *The Charlie Rose Show*, not to mention a recent talk they did in China that reached 195 million people via social media within thirty minutes. They used that talk to call for a referendum to ban ivory imports into China, and within six months President Xi and President Obama agreed on ivory bans.

Despite such fame, the Jouberts are humble. Their work is about protecting wilderness, and, as such, their greatest rewards are not monetary. Their greatest rewards are their conservation successes. As Beverly says, "We won't stop until we have done everything in our power to conserve Africa's wildlife for future generations." And it's that next generation of wilderness advocates that are the key to ensuring the future of ecosystems across the globe. "It's important right now for all of us, young and old, not to be complacent and take it for granted that someone else is protecting the remaining wilderness areas," Beverly says. "If we stop taking action right now, we'll lose these unique ecosystems forever. That's why it's so important to educate young people and ignite their passion for wildlife as leaders and custodians of tomorrow. We must give them hope, arm them with knowledge, and show them how they too can, and must, make a difference."

Beverly and Dereck Joubert, two people that President Khama of Botswana refers to as "real children of Africa," are making a difference. Using their filmmaking skills as a voice for advocacy and education, they are bringing the heart of wild Africa to the world, exposing the global community to what we stand to lose and why we must work together to save it.

For more information on Beverly and Dereck Joubert, please visit www.Wildlifefilms.co and www.greatplainsfoundation.com.

CHAPTER 3

Anne Innis Dagg, PhD: Necks' Best Thing

"Whatever I wanted to do, I just went and did it."

—Dr. Anne Innis Dagg

Anne Innis Dagg.

BIOLOGIST. GIRAFFE RESEARCHER. FEMINIST. PIONEER. These are just a few words that could be used to describe Anne Innis Dagg, a woman who in 2016, at age eighty-three, largely defies categorization. But there is one thing about her that can be simply stated: her love of giraffes.

Anne Innis first saw giraffes when she was visiting Chicago's Brookfield Zoo as a young child. "It was love at first sight," she says, recalling the experience of seeing the elegant animals that had cantered across their enclosure toward her. "I was entranced." From that day on, Anne had a goal: to study giraffes in the wild and learn everything she could about them. For a girl born in Toronto in 1933, though, the path to becoming a giraffe researcher was far from straightforward. When she was a teenager, there had been no formal studies done on the animal, no protocol for how to conduct field research on African wildlife, nobody before her to turn to and ask. To make matters worse, she was a girl, and for girls, such a thing as studying a wild animal on the other side of the world was seemingly impossible.

But Anne somehow made it possible, and, as such, pioneered the study of giraffes.

🐾

There are believed to be nine subspecies of giraffes (*Giraffa camelopardalis*) found in twenty-one African countries from Niger to Central and East Africa and down to South Africa. With new genetic data, however, there is evidence to suggest that some of these subspecies might in fact be true species. While the concept of species can be seen merely as a taxonomic exercise in "splitting and lumping"—separating subspecies out into new species or grouping them into a single species—knowing taxonomy is important in planning conservation strategies for an iconic animal whose populations have dropped as much as 40 percent in the last two decades. According to the Giraffe Conservation Foundation, with the exception of the Angolan, South, and West African giraffes, all other subspecies populations are either decreasing or unstable. The usual mix of environmental issues—from habitat loss and fragmentation to human population growth and poaching to civil war and unrest—is harming giraffes. To make conservation more difficult, these herbivores, standing up to seventeen feet in height and weighing up to 2,800 pounds, require a large area to survive.

In 1956, at age twenty-three, when Anne set out alone for South Africa, neither she nor anyone else knew any of this about giraffes. All she knew was that their large brown eyes, willowy charm, and slow-moving grace captivated her.

🐾

Anne grew up in a middle-class family, the youngest of four children. Her father, Harold Innis, was a well-known professor of economic history at the University of Toronto, and her mother, Mary Quayle Innis, was an author and a homemaker and later became Dean of Women at University College of the University of Toronto. One of the highlights of Anne's family life was the two-month summer holidays they spent most years in Footes Bay, Muskoka in a rented cottage, which she recalls would have been an ideal place to study nature had anyone in her family known much about the plants or animals. For high school, she attended the private Bishop Strachan School for girls. Although she learned nothing about giraffes or other mammals while in attendance, she recalls her five years there as wonderful.

After high school, Anne entered the University of Toronto's Honors Science Program. The heavy workload was not a problem, but some of her courses in zoology were disappointing. "It was sometimes about collecting and preparing specimens," she says. "So many animals were killed. It filled me with revulsion."

During one of her summers at university, a few of her male classmates were hired by a professor to drive across eastern Canada and trap and collect animals such as deer mice (two species), white-footed mice, house mice, jumping mice, and five kinds of shrews, then prepare skins for study. Women students, though, even those with top marks, were never allowed to take part in such field trips. Anne hoped to be able to do outdoor research to gain environmental experience, so she expanded the scope of her job search. "Several summers I applied to be a fire ranger in northern Ontario, but, again, women were judged unsuitable for such jobs and never hired. Instead, I worked at the Royal Ontario Museum, cleaning mammal skulls with tweezers for much less money."

While she was in her second year of university, her father died, which was a huge setback for Anne. Despite her emotional trauma, the lack of opportunity for women, and the often-difficult classes, Anne graduated with top honors in 1955, determined to set out for Africa and pursue her interest in giraffes. "I wrote to a number of people, including Louis Leakey, to ask about ways and means of studying giraffes in the wild, but no one was encouraging," she says. (Although Leakey did write back to Anne and try to help, he could not come up with a place for her to observe giraffes.) "They gave instead reasons why I couldn't, and shouldn't, come to Africa." The reasons given: a "girl" wouldn't be able to do such work alone. The rhinos were too fierce. There was no money for such a study.

In other words, a dead end.

But Anne did not "do" dead ends.

If she couldn't get to Africa, she decided she would continue with her studies. "I finally enrolled in the master's program at the University of Toronto to study the genetics of mice so that I wouldn't waste a year," she says. She had become greatly interested in inheritance in mammals, but she says she also chose the subject because it was one of the few thesis topics that did not involve hurting live animals in some way. She completed her degree in 1956, and this time when she set out to plan a trip to Africa, she was not going to take no for an answer.

Anne started an extensive letter-writing campaign, looking for a place she could do research. A fellow graduate student, Rufus Churcher, told her about two of his earlier professors, Griff and Jakes Ewer, who at that time were at Rhodes University in Grahamstown, South Africa. Churcher said that the couple, who were originally from Great Britain, might be able to help her. "I contacted them, and Jakes put me in touch with Mr. Matthew, a farmer in the Eastern Transvaal, who might be willing to allow a student to do research on his 20,000-acre ranch where ninety-five giraffe lived among the cattle," says Anne. "I wrote to him immediately, giving only my initials rather than my first name. He wrote back, assuming that I was a man, to say he would be willing to have me stay there to study the behavior of his giraffes."

With a place to stay in South Africa, a cash prize awarded for her studies, money she had earned during her university years, and a top-up from her mother, all Anne had to do was figure out how she would actually study giraffes once she was there. "I asked my professors what books to read, and they had no idea," she says. "Nobody had ever done this before. The only book they could recommend was on a herd of red deer that had been studied in Scotland, but that was twenty years earlier and involved the shooting of individual animals, so it had little to do with what I wanted to accomplish." She would have to figure out methods for studying giraffes in the wild on her own.

In 1956, Anne Innis, a twenty-three-year-old Canadian woman, who by all societal expectations should stay home and get married, boarded an ocean liner for London. After waiting in London for an available spot on a ship for Africa, she set out on the two-week trip to Port Elizabeth for an unprecedented adventure that would come to define the study and knowledge of giraffes. "I arrived in Grahamstown,

South Africa, in the summer of 1956," says Anne. "The Ewers had no real idea of who I was, but they treated me with kindness by giving me advice and full board for my first weeks in Africa."

It was while with the Ewers that Anne encountered her first obstacle on African soil. Before boarding the ship from London to Africa, she had written to Mr. Matthew, informing him, among other things, of her gender. She recalls what happened next:

> In Grahamstown, to my horror, the second letter I had from Mr. Matthew stated that he had to withdraw his offer of support because I was a "girl." He was sorry that I had needlessly come so far, but was sure I would understand that he had no place for me, since his wife and daughters were out of the country, and I would have had to stay at his house. I wrote back begging him to reconsider his refusal—I could stay in a nearby hospital, or in a tent, or even in my new-to-me car, a Ford Prefect I called Camelo (for the generic name of the giraffe, *Camelopardalis*), which I bought second-hand. Finally, Mr. Matthew changed his mind, and decided I could stay with him for four months and for my room and board I could do some typing for him and keep a record of the species of bushes and trees browsed by his huge herd of cattle.

As soon as she received Matthew's letter, Anne set out alone in Camelo to drive the thousand miles to Fleur de Lys, his ranch. She was advised to make the trip, sometimes along unpaved country roads, in four days. She decided to do it in two. The journey went well—until near midnight the second night when her car broke down. "I was within a few miles of the ranch and decided to walk along the deserted dirt road in pitch blackness," she says. As she walked, something occurred to her: snakes. Not just any snakes—poisonous puff adders, such as those she'd seen run over on the roads, and deadly black mambas—venomous creatures she'd heard about, but never seen. To add to her fear of serpents, she was terrified at the thought of leopards, lions, and drunken men as she walked on her own without even a flashlight. "I was infinitely relieved to reach the ranch and meet Mr. Matthew!"

The next afternoon, after she had oriented herself to the stunning view of the Drakensberg Mountains, Mr. Matthew, a kind man, but an imposing figure at over six feet tall, took Anne to see her first wild giraffe. "We drove along and there was a giraffe coming to drink in a small pool," she recalls. "It was the most beautiful animal I'd ever seen."

For the next four months, Anne documented the ecology and behavior of the ninety-five giraffes that lived on Mr. Matthew's ranch. Every morning, seven days a week, she'd wake up at 5 a.m. and, after a cup of tea, set out to the field for two hours of early observation. So as not to interfere with their natural behavior, she'd sit in her small car and observe the giraffes, writing down every five minutes what they were up to. After breakfast she would spend the rest of the day in the field, with a short break for lunch, until it grew dark at about 6 p.m.

Anne's main equipment was a pair of binoculars Mr. Matthew had lent her, her camera, and a notebook. She would especially watch the activities of a few recognizable individuals. There was Star, a male giraffe she named for his star-shaped spots. There was Pom Pom. There were the twins—each giraffe an individual that Anne got to know. One thing about these animals she found particularly striking was their walking gait. "They seemed to float," she says. "Two right legs moving forward, then two left legs."

Besides the mechanics of their gait (that she filmed using Mr. Matthew's 16 mm camera, and later analyzed in detail), Anne noted two interesting giraffe behaviors. One of those behaviors is called flehmen, which, she explains, "is when a male collects some urine from a female adult in his mouth and can tell from this if she will be ready to mate. If she is in heat, he will mount her, and if she is coming into heat, he will wait around for a day or so and then mate with her."

The second behavior she noted was homosexuality in male giraffes. "One time from my car I was watching two male giraffes fighting, hitting the body of the other with his horns. Then they were rubbing their heads together until one went behind the other and mounted him," she explains. Anne was too embarrassed to tell Mr. Matthew what she had seen, but years later when people were insisting that homosexual behavior was unnatural, she carried out a study, searching through books and scientific articles and locating over one hundred species in which homosexual behavior had been documented. She became the first researcher to publish a comprehensive paper in a scientific journal about homosexual behavior in animals. "People were excited to see the topic out in the open," she says. "The data proved that it was wrong for anti-gay people to assert that homosexuality was unnatural—obviously it was very much a part of animal nature."

After four months, the time frame she'd been offered to stay with Mr. Matthew (not knowing he actually wanted her to stay on longer), Anne set off again on her own to find areas further north where she could observe other races of giraffes, but without success. To replenish her finances, she worked briefly as a typist in Dar es Salaam, Tanganyika (now Tanzania), then climbed Mt. Kilimanjaro as an adventure, travelled alone to Nairobi, and searched out several other areas in East Africa where giraffes might be observed. Eventually she met up again with Mr. Matthew for a brief visit to Victoria Falls, after which she returned to Fleur de Lys to complete her giraffe observations.

In 1957, at age twenty-four, with her year in Africa a success, Anne believed she had a promising career as an academic ahead of her. She was a seasoned traveler, was soon to publish a number of scientific papers, and was the world's expert on giraffes. At home in Canada, though, her path would prove to be anything but easy.

Shortly before Anne left for Africa, her friend Ian Dagg, a Canadian physicist, asked her to marry him. Not wanting to let anything get in the way of her expedition, she asked him to wait until she returned. While in London, on her way home by ship from South Africa, she made good on her promise and they were married. The couple returned to Ottawa, Canada, where she tried to find a job in biology, with no success. "Neither of the local universities wanted to hire me, nor did the National Museum," Anne remembers. "I spent the fall working at a temporary job at Carleton University and in my spare time writing what I planned to be the definitive book on the giraffe." In 1959, the Daggs moved to Waterloo, Ontario, where her husband became a professor of physics at the University of Waterloo. It was while they were there that she began to appreciate the sexual discrimination facing women in academia.

Anne ultimately desired to be an academic like her husband, so even though she was raising three young children, she started teaching one course per year at Waterloo Lutheran University (now Wilfrid Laurier University). Her teaching went so well that she was asked to teach a second course, just as the other two male members of the small biology department were doing. "I happily thought I would be full-time, but no," she says. "The men were full-time, but I would remain part-time and poorly paid, even though I had the same teaching load and was publishing more research papers—this time on facets of the giraffe such as their food preferences, sub-speciation, and distribution."

In 1965, Anne decided to stop teaching and to earn her PhD in biology at the University of Waterloo in order to "give herself maximum qualifications for being a professor." She mostly worked on her dissertation at home where she could keep an eye on her children and *their* locomotion, while analyzing the locomotion of large wild mammals:

> By borrowing wildlife films from the Canadian Broadcasting Corporation and other sources, I could work largely at home while minding the children. I organized a scheme whereby I could analyze sequences of individual animals walking, pacing, and galloping and note which of their feet were on the ground in each frame. After studying many thousands of frames of giraffe, pronghorn, and various species of deer and antelope, I was able to show that the way their four legs moved during their gaits varied with such things as size, shape, speed, and habitat.

The entire time Anne was writing the dissertation for her PhD (which she managed to earn in two years) and raising children, she was also collecting information for her giraffe book. While working on the book, Anne had many other experiences—both positive and negative—including teaching at the University of Guelph ("I got turned down for tenure in 1972 despite twenty published scientific papers and having an excellent record of teaching"), studying the locomotion of camels in Mauritania with German scientist Hilde Gauthier-Pilters ("in 1981, shortly before Hilde died of breast cancer, we coauthored a highly praised book on the camel"), getting passed over for yet another teaching job at the University of Waterloo ("the dean of science told me that he would never give tenure to a married woman"), publishing additional papers on giraffes and other animals, living with her family for a year in Australia while her husband had a sabbatical, and using the Sydney Zoo and its giraffes and other animals to observe and write more scientific papers.

Throughout these years, Anne never stopped gathering information for her giraffe book. Hearing about the book she was planning, Bristol Foster, a former classmate from the University of Toronto, sent her data he had collected over three years, but had not had time to analyze, on the giraffes of the Nairobi National Park. "These new results were so exciting that they gave me new impetus for my giraffe manuscript," says Anne. "I asked Foster to coauthor the book, which meant that we incorporated all his data, and that his excellent photographs could serve as illustrations." The book, *The Giraffe: Its Biology, Behavior and Ecology*, published in 1976 and reprinted in 1982, is still, in 2016, considered by many to be the Bible in the field of giraffe conservation.

In 1978, students hired Anne as a part-time resource person in the student-run Integrated Studies program (later changed to Independent Studies) at the University of Waterloo, a position she held until August 2016, when the program closed. "It was one of the best things that ever happened to me," she says about getting hired. "It has radically affected the way I think and what I think about. The program attracted a wide variety of students, some incredibly right wing, most very left, lesbians, gay men, Natives, goof-offs, specialists, and generalists. Many of my stereotyped beliefs that I held since birth have been destroyed. It has been wonderful."

While Anne was teaching and publishing books and papers on topics ranging from feminism to Canadian mammals to animal rights, she never stopped loving giraffes. But after publishing their book in 1976, her life with giraffes slowed down—it was not until 2010, when Anne was seventy-seven years old—that it again gained momentum. On February 4 of that year, the International Association of Giraffe Care Professionals recognized Anne for her pioneering work. Following this award, when asked by University of Cambridge Press to write another book on giraffes, she published *Giraffe: Biology, Behavior and Conservation* in 2014.

It was an occasion in May 2016, though, that Anne calls her proudest moment. She was asked to return to the Brookfield Zoo, where she had seen her first giraffe as a child, to receive another award. "At the International Giraffid Conference (which included okapi as well as giraffe) they gave a lifetime achievement award in giraffe science to me," she says. "From now on, the award, called the 'Anne Innis Dagg Award,' will be given to a deserving giraffe conservationist every two years. I was in tears when they told me, I was so moved."

Propelled by her long overdue recognition and introduction to contemporary giraffe researchers, Anne returned to Africa in 2014 and again in 2016 to visit her tall, charming friends in the wild. She had not been back to see wild giraffes since 1957. "It has been wonderful," she says. "Getting back into the world of giraffes again has just made me so happy."

Having written twenty-one books and sixty scientific papers, Anne has never slowed down, given up, or stopped trying. If she couldn't find a publisher, she simply published her own books. If she couldn't find a job, she created one. If she couldn't find someone to fund her research, she funded it herself. With over six decades of drive and determination, Anne offers the following advice about conservation: "Never say never. Do what you have to do. Insist." Looking back on her time in Africa and her pioneering work and adventure, Anne says, "I didn't think of myself as brave. I just desperately wanted to do it."

Never giving up, insisting, and not letting anybody stop her are all part of the Anne Innis Dagg legacy; the other part of her legacy is on behalf of giraffes. Anne has offered the world insight into their behavior and ecology, findings that a new generation of researchers can use to help this unique animal survive. She has reintroduced to the world these magnificent and loveable giants, spreading the word of their plight before it is too late.

For more information on Anne Innis Dagg, please see www.annedagg.net.

CHAPTER 4

Yossi Leshem, PhD: Using Birds as Peacemakers in the Middle East

"Migrating Birds Know No Boundaries."

—Prof. Yossi Leshem

Credit: Hagai Aharon

Yossi Leshen.

WHEN A GRIFFON VULTURE WEARING a GPS locator, strapped on by researcher Or Spiegel from the Hebrew University in Jerusalem, landed in Saudi Arabia in 2011, officials thought the bird was an Israeli Mossad spy. Suspicious of the data the GPS device was collecting, the Saudis detained the vulture, claiming that the Zionists had trained the bird for espionage. (After several weeks, the Saudi officials determined the vulture indeed was just a migrating bird and not an informant, and they let it go.)

Finding common ground in the Middle East is not easy, but Professor Yossi Leshem believes birds can build bridges and unite enemies. "I have a vision of Middle East peace that includes birds bringing people together," says Leshem, Israel's most famous ornithologist. Whereas the alleged "Mossad vulture" highlights the difficulty of such ambitions, other birds such as barn owls, migrating storks, and even other raptors have been uniting Jews, Palestinians, and Jordanians through cross-cultural collaborations. These collaborations, started by Leshem twenty years ago, bring together people on opposite sides of a political divide to protect wildlife and the environment.

Currently working as a professor at the Department of Zoology at Tel Aviv University and as the director of the International Center for the Study of Bird Migration at Latrun (of which he is the founder), fifteen miles west of Jerusalem, Leshem is Israel's unofficial ambassador for birds. You can't say the words "bird" and "Israel" without evoking Yossi Leshem, who wants people to know Israel for something other than its archeological, religious, and historic sites and its political conflict. Birds may be just that thing.

Located at the juncture of three continents, Israel is a bottleneck for bird migration, funneling 500 million birds between Europe, Asia, and Africa down the 4,400-mile Great Rift Valley each spring and autumn. Of 280 different migrating species that use the Israeli land bridge, thirty-five different raptors, numbering in the hundreds of thousands of individual birds, rely on the uplift of thermal currents created by the sun heating the land to migrate. With such colossal numbers, Israel is a mecca for birds and bird lovers alike. Besides the sheer numbers, there is also biodiversity. Many birds, such as the striated scops owl, the sooty falcon, and the desert tawny owl, reach the boundary of their distribution in Israel. Five hundred and forty different species can be seen in Israel, even though it is a small country.

However, with the mass migration come problems such as instances of airplane-bird collisions. It was his role in mapping migration and reducing such collisions that put Leshem on the map.

Leshem was born in the Israeli city of Haifa in 1947 to parents who had escaped from Nazi Germany. It was his mother, Klara Loffelholz, who had fled from Frankfurt am Main in 1933, who initially introduced him to nature. "She couldn't tell a donkey from a bird," Leshem jokes, fondly recounting his mother's Friday outings with her two sons. "She just liked to hike. She took us to the top of Mount Carmel and asked us to breathe deeply because she had the feeling that the air in Haifa was polluted. Because of her I started to love nature."

It was not just nature he loved, but flight. Anything that flew captured young Leshem's interest. When he was in secondary school, he could look skyward and identify every Israeli Air Force plane by name. "I wanted to become a pilot in the Israeli Air Force," he says. At age seventeen, that dream was thwarted when he got glasses. Because you couldn't be a pilot if you wore glasses, when it came time for military service, Leshem joined the army instead. Little did he know, despite his eyeglasses and poor vision, birds and airplanes would eventually become his life.

After studying the Bonelli's eagle for his master's degree, Leshem wanted to study the lappet-faced vulture for his PhD. In 1979, there were just five pairs of these birds left in Israel. Leshem's first thought was to set up feeding stations for the vulture, but it was too late. In 1980 there was just one pair left in Israel, and by 1986 the Israeli population went extinct. Leshem needed a new subject for his dissertation, and it was at this time he learned about the problems associated with birds and aircrafts.

"In three decades, the Israeli Air Force had suffered seventy-five crashes and lost eleven aircraft due to collisions with birds. Three pilots were killed," Leshem explains. The problem became even worse in 1982 when Israel gave the Sinai back to Egypt, and as a result their training airspace narrowed and became more concentrated in the path of millions of migrating birds. Leshem told the Air Force he'd like to study the situation and find a way to reduce the number of collisions. At first the Air Force denied him—with all of Israel's security concerns, birds were not a priority. A few months later, though, a honey buzzard destroyed a five-million-dollar Skyhawk plane flying near Hebron (the honey buzzard penetrated the aircraft, hitting the ejection handle, and the pilot was ejected, his neck and vertebra broken), and Major General Amos Lapidot (the Commander of the Air Force at the time) called Leshem and asked for his help.

To understand the problem, Leshem initially enlisted the assistance of about sixty bird watchers across the country per year. But he soon realized ground data wasn't adequate. He'd have to take to the sky. His initial attempt at soaring with the birds was in a Cessna 206, a light, single-engine plane. He did twenty-nine flights with the Cessna, mapping major migration routes over Israel. The light aircraft, however, turned out to have several problems, including the fact that the engine noise scared the soaring birds, and its high speed and large circling radius made it impossible to track a single flock. He then tried a hang glider and an ultra-light airplane, but neither allowed him to stay with the birds for long enough to collect sufficient data.

In 1985, Leshem found a solution: a motorized glider manufactured in Poland that could fit two people and spend nine continuous hours in the air. "The idea," he explains, "is that you take off and then cut the engine and fly wingtip-to-wingtip with migrating birds for five to ten hours a day. This is something not many people had done." Leshem did it for 272 days. While in the sky, Leshem flew with tens of thousands of storks, eagles, pelicans, and honey buzzards, always "attaching" the glider to a single flock and escorting it along its entire flight route from the Lebanese to the Egyptian border in autumn and vice versa in the spring migration, a distance of about 250 miles. "It's so quiet in the air with no engine," he says. "You feel like a bird. It's so inspiring."

After five years of data collection, Leshem found that twice each year birds used three main "superhighways" across Israel. He was able to get detailed information on migratory routes, passage times, velocity, and altitude of the soaring birds. The Israeli Air Force estimates that Leshem's study has saved Israel over one billion dollars, reduced bird-aircraft collisions by 76 percent, and saved the life of numerous pilots and birds. Of everything he has accomplished, it is of this that he is proudest. "According to the Jewish sources," he explains, "if you succeed in saving the life of one person, you save the entire world."

Leshem's work on reducing aircraft-bird collisions is just one achievement he is famous for. He is also well known and loved for other aspects of conservation, especially that of regional cooperation in avian research. The story of regional cooperation began with a meeting in Bethlehem in 1995 when Leshem and his friend Imad Atrash, Director of the Palestine Wildlife Society, had a vision of "Cooperation between Israelis and Palestinians in the field of birds." In 1996, Leshem received funds from the German Ministry of the Environment in cooperation with Professor Peter Berthold from the Max Planck Institute in Radolfzell, Germany, from Tel Aviv University, and from the Society for the Protection of Nature in Israel to fit 120 migrating German white storks with satellite transmitters, so they could be tracked from Germany via the Middle East to Africa. The Israeli Ministry of Education then funded a website and curriculum so that students could follow the migrating birds, and each individual stork was given a Jewish, Christian, or Muslim name, such as David, Princessa, or Fatima. In 1998, USAID got involved, pitching in 1.5 million dollars, and within two years, the project called Migrating Birds Know No Boundaries had two hundred Israeli schools, thirty Palestinian schools, and thirty Jordanian schools participating.

Even Al Gore was impressed. When the former US vice president came to Israel in 1999 to sign a contract with the Minister of Education for the Israeli government to join his GLOBE project (which sought to connect five thousand schools across the world to communicate about water and air pollution via the Internet) Leshem got to meet with him. "I told him that migrating birds know no boundaries," says Leshem. "He and a few people of his staff got totally excited! They said, 'Wow, the Israelis did it again! The idea that migrating birds know no boundaries is much more exciting than pollution of water and air!'"

The Migrating Birds Know No Boundaries project didn't just teach students about birds; it also taught them about each other. When they met in the field, groups of Palestinians (both Muslims and Christians), Israeli Jews, and Israeli Arabs would eat lunch together, and, as kids have the remarkable ability to do when given the chance, they became friends. Despite complications related to things such as entry permits and blockades, the project worked. It worked so well, in fact, that in 1998, five thousand Jewish, Arab, and Palestinian schoolchildren gathered at Latrun to learn about the birds that migrate over their countries. The project was going extremely well until 2000, when the second Intifada broke out.

The violence and unrest almost destroyed the project—leaders were forced to meet in Cyprus and Turkey, the closest safe regions, and the students could no longer get together. Still, in their individual classrooms, the project continued until 2004. Students, though no longer in touch with each other, studied birds, and project leaders communicated weekly via telephone and email. "In the future, when the students can meet again, they will do so," says Leshem. "When peace comes, we will expand this educational work and run joint operations to invite tourists to bird centers—three in Jordan, three in Palestine, and ten in Israel."

Migrating Birds Know No Boundaries is not Leshem's only regional collaboration. He also works with Jordanians and Palestinians to use barn owls as a means of biological pest control in agriculture. After the founding of the state of Israel in 1948, the Zionist motto was "Build and be built," a motto that led to rapid development in the country's early years. Development spelled ecological disaster, especially in the Hula Valley in northern Israel, where fifteen thousand acres of wetlands were drained to make way for farmland, and vast amounts of pesticides were applied to grow crops such as alfalfa. With the spike in pesticides came a sharp decline in birds of prey due to the effects of feeding on poisoned rodents and suffering from secondary poisoning.

Instead of using poison to kill rodents, Leshem thought owls might do the job. In a 1983 pilot project at Kibbutz Sde Eliyahu (the leading kibbutz in Israel for organic agriculture), Leshem and his colleagues put up nesting boxes. They discovered that the boxes attracted many pairs of barn owls that were desperately looking for nesting sites. A single pair of barn owls can raise between two and twelve chicks and eat from two thousand to six thousand mice a year, thus reducing, if not eliminating, the need for poisonous agrochemicals. After two decades, they also started to use ammunition boxes, which were recycled into nesting boxes with support from the army.

In 2002, Mansour Abu-Rashid, a renowned Jordanian general who once fought against Israel, but who later became a proponent of nonviolence, playing a central role in the 1994 peace process, came to a seminar at Kibbutz Sde Eliyahu to learn about the barn owl project. At first he and Jordanian farmers were skeptical because, for some Muslims, owls portend evil. When they learned about the achievements in Israel, though, they decided to try. Imad Atrash attended this same seminar and decided that he too wanted to expand the project into the Palestinian Authority.

The United States government (USAID, MERC), along with the European Union, the Hanns Seidel Foundation, the Israeli Ministry for Regional Cooperation, the Ministry of Foreign Affairs, the Ministry of Agriculture, and the Ministry of Environmental Protection, financed the collaboration. Over the next ten years, Leshem helped run seminars for farmers, researchers, conservationists, and students, while Atrash and Abu-Rashid spearheaded the publication of booklets in Arabic on how to do this work. Since the project's inception, about three hundred farmers have come from the Palestinian Authority in the West Bank and from Jordan to learn about how owls can help farmers and lessen environmental impact. "Today (in 2016) we have three thousand nesting boxes in Israel, about 220 in Jordan, and about two hundred in Palestine in the West Bank," says Leshem. (And in the 1990s, the wetlands of the Hula Valley were re-flooded. The freshwater, along with peanuts planted by the farmers, began to attract thousands of cranes. "The cranes are like Israelis. They are very noisy, they like to be together, and they eat peanuts and chickpeas," Leshem said in a 2011 article in the magazine *Moment*, which covers Jewish politics, culture, and religion.)

These sorts of projects help wildlife while allowing people to forget politics and speak the common language of conservation. One moment of communication, this time nonverbal, stands out strongly for Leshem. "In 2015, we were at a seminar in Jordan on a mountain overlooking the Dead Sea where you could see the sunset of Israel," he says. "As we summed up the lectures, all of a sudden everyone started to dance together: Jordanians, Palestinians, and Israelis. I thought, wow, it works, people are coming together. If you listen to the politicians, you are pessimistic and think nothing works here."

Leshem's love of his country and of birds led him to another national project. For Israel's sixtieth anniversary in 2008, Leshem, with his partner Dan Alon, Director of the Israel Ornithological Center, came up with the idea of choosing a national bird. "I wanted everyone to talk of birds," he says. And people did just that; over a five-month contest, soldiers, school children, online communities, and members of the general public engaged in discussions about bulbuls, lesser kestrels, griffon vultures, Palestine sunbirds, and hoopoes. After 1.1 million votes were cast, the ninth president of Israel, Shimon Peres (while alive, a fellow nature lover and friend of Leshem), announced the winner: the hoopoe, a medium-sized black-and-white bird with an orange-feathered mohawk. News of the winner wasn't just confined to Israel; in a June 2008 episode of *The Colbert Report*, host Stephen Colbert wished the Israelis luck with their new national bird, saying: "Congratulations, Israel. Just as America soars like the mighty eagle, may you emulate the noble long-billed hoopoe by squirting fecal matter at intruders."

In addition to running national campaigns, working at a university, and directing bird centers across Israel, Leshem has written three books, published hundreds of scientific papers and popular articles, and received over a dozen conservation awards. Three awards in particular stand out for Leshem. In 2005, he received the Mike Kuhring Prize from the International Bird Strike Committee for his achievements in improving flight safety and for his mission to connect safety with nature conservation. In 2008, Israel's Minister of the Environment and President Peres gave Leshem a Lifetime Achievement Award for Environmental Protection and named him one of Israel's top ten environmentalists as part of Israel's sixtieth anniversary. He received the Bruno H. Schubert Foundation Award for World Nature Conservation in 2012. And when former American President Jimmy Carter (another presidential bird lover) visited Israel in 2005, he devoted two-and-a-half pages in his book about the Middle East to Leshem and Imad Atrash, who hosted him, calling them "the Jacques Cousteau of birds."

To achieve so much and also have a family (currently at five children and seven grandchildren), Leshem says, "I'm very narrow-minded. My main mission in life is to take care of birds and the conservation of habitat. Maybe I am also a good lecturer and I know how to get people excited. When people see that you are excited and care about what you do, they listen to you."

Leshem offers the 2016 Davos World Economic Forum (in which he arranged a talk in collaboration with Professor Alexandre Roulin from the University of Lausanne, Switzerland) as an example of how his enthusiasm sparks others. "Everybody said don't go there, who will listen to your stories of birds? These are the leaders of the world. We said no. We want to go." Leshem and Roulin, along with friends Mansour Abu-Rashid and General Baruch Spiegel (the Israeli partner of General Mansour, both of whom played a role in the 1994 Peace Treaty with Jordan) attended the conference. Shimon Peres was supposed to attend as well, but he had a mild heart attack and his son, Chemi Peres, managing director and co-founder of Pitango Venture Capital and chairman of the Peres Center for Peace, attended in his place. After Leshem's delegation presented their program "Birds Know No Boundaries—Cross-Border Environmental Projects in the Middle East for People and Nature," Shimon Peres called Leshem. "He was so impressed. He said everyone was excited about your event."

Most of Leshem's work is science and education, but he knows the arts are another tool to connect people with the natural world and conservation. "I believe if you want to succeed in conservation, you have to go in two directions: one direction is the brain, which is science and studies, the other is the heart, which is music and art," he explains. "You also have to get people out in the field. If I want to convince a decision-maker of something, I don't use papers. I take them out where they can touch and feel and see, and suddenly they get excited."

Leshem's close friend and seven-time Grammy award winner, musician Paul Winter, is one artist who understands this connection to the heart. After flying for three hours in a glider from the north to the desert with three thousand white storks, he composed a ninety-minute piece called *Flyways* about the migration of birds from Europe through Israel to South Africa, which he played parts of at Davos in 2016. "I am sure he will get his eighth Grammy for it," says Leshem.

Although there are still conservation issues, including poisoning by farmers, destruction of habitat, hunting, rappelling near raptor nests, high voltage power lines and electrocution, and conflicts between fishermen and pelicans and cormorants, Leshem is ultimately hopeful about the state of birds in Israel. "We are marathon runners," he says. "You can't solve problems in a year or in a decade. You have to work on it long term and then you succeed." To solve problems and to make sure the next generation of Israelis works toward conservation, he believes strongly in education and considers himself an educator as much as a researcher. Leshem is more than an educator, though. He is a mentor to the nation. Thanks largely to his advocacy, charisma, single-mindedness, and passion, people throughout Israel are now carrying out bird-related projects on their own. "In March 2016, in the village of Mazkeret Batya, they put up 150 pictures of birds with their names on all the road electricity boxes so people could learn about birds," says Leshem. "I wasn't part of this, but I was really proud to see that they did this with their own initiatve."

It's not only Israelis he'd like to see interested in his nation's birds; it's the one hundred million other birders throughout the world. With more bird-watching comes more birds, as ecotourism money can be funneled back into conservation projects such as the reintroduction of four endangered vulture species—griffon, lappet-faced, Egyptian, and bearded—to the Middle East. Tourists can even fly with the birds in a motorized glider like the one Leshem used for his dissertation. "Israel has five of them. It's a life experience," he says. "You are flying closer to God with the birds."

Perhaps, through birds, people are getting closer to each other, too. Like the biblical white dove and the olive branch—or these days the barn owl—Leshem and the birds he loves are helping spread peace, one bird lover at a time.

For more information on Yossi Leshem, please visit www.birds.org.il.

CHAPTER 5

· · ·

Laurie Marker, PhD:
Cheetahs' Best Friend

"I don't allow any negativity to stop the course of my work. I can't allow anything to affect my inspiration, because the cheetah doesn't have time."

—Laurie Marker

Laurie Marker.

I T WAS GOATS THAT LED Dr. Laurie Marker to cheetahs.

In 1973, at age nineteen, when Marker moved from Napa Valley, California to Roseburg, Oregon to start a vineyard, she brought her dairy goats with her. Understanding the positive effect animals have on children, she offered to donate two of her goat kids to Wildlife Safari, a drive-through wild animal park that also had a children's zoo. While at the park, she found out they were looking for help. Having grown up on a small farm

39

surrounded by horses, dogs, and goats, Marker was hired on the spot to run the Safari's veterinary clinic and animal nursery (she had some pre-veterinary training at San Francisco State University) and also to head their children's zoo. Her role at Wildlife Safari involved caring for animals that needed special attention, including those that had been orphaned. "I raised many different animals including guanacos, monkeys, boas, goats, and lions," she says. "Then I met a cheetah cub named Khayam who had been born at the Safari, and I was allowed to care for her. One look into her deep, amber eyes and I was in love. Little did I know," says Marker, "that looking into Khayam's eyes would change my life."

Marker set out to learn as much as she could about cheetahs, but the answers she received were incomplete. In the 1970s, all people really understood about them were that they were difficult to breed in captivity, they had a short life span, and the species' numbers were dropping. The lack of information led Marker to an obvious conclusion: she would become the cheetah expert and fill in the blanks herself.

In 1977, Marker traveled to Namibia, the country where Khayam's parents had come from. Here, she conducted a first-of-its-kind research project to see if a captive-born cub, her beloved Khayam, could be taught to hunt in the wild. "The experiment was a great success," Marker says. "Khayam learned to catch antelope on her own, but the experience also taught me that learning to hunt was not the only critical part of living in the wild for a cheetah." Khayam didn't just need to learn *to* hunt; she had to avoid *being* hunted because, as Marker learned, farmers were killing hundreds of cheetahs yearly, as they considered them a threat to their livestock. This realization meant that Khayam would likely not survive in the wild, so Marker brought her friend back home to Oregon where the two lived together until Khayam's death in 1986. In their shared life, Khayam became an ambassador for her species, travelling around the United States with Marker, meeting schoolchildren, appearing on TV shows throughout the country, including programs such as *The Johnny Carson Show* and *The Today Show*, and educating the world about cheetahs. "She was an amazing friend," says Marker.

Besides working with Khayam, Marker spent the 1980s developing the most successful cheetah breeding program in the United States and the third most successful in the world. She also developed the National (1982) and the International (1988) Cheetah Studbook and the

Cheetah Species Survival Plan (SSP) (in 1985) to begin a management plan for the captive cheetah population. From 1988 to 1990, she was the executive director of the NOAHS (New Opportunities in Animal Health Science) Center at the National Zoo of the Smithsonian Institute in Washington, DC, where many cheetah research collaborations were developed. During these years, though, wild cheetahs and Namibia were never far from Marker's heart.

In 1990, a little over a decade after her first trip to Namibia (she had gone back many times since 1977 and developed relationships with local people), the country gained independence and was freed of apartheid. Marker had not considered living in Namibia under the oppressive colonial government, but once the political situation changed, she decided to give up her comfortable American life, move to Africa, and dedicate her life to saving wild cheetahs. On April 1, 1990, with two dogs and fourteen crates filled with research equipment, Marker moved to Namibia for good. "I liquidated my small personal assets, which paid for the move—all of fifteen thousand US dollars," she says, as if leaving behind everything familiar for the unknown in Africa was no big deal, something anyone might do. She then used what money she had left to set up shop in a borrowed farmhouse in Otijiwarongo, three hours north of Windhoek, Namibia's capital, and start the Cheetah Conservation Fund (CCF).

🐾

The world cheetah population has dropped from 100,000 to ten thousand over the past one hundred years. While the story of their population decline is similar to that of other species across the globe—loss of natural habitat worsened by climate change—two of the challenges cheetahs face are unique.

Ironically, one such challenge has to do with the cheetah's greatest asset: its speed. A cheetah can accelerate to seventy miles per hour in just three seconds. With special claws that work like cleats; a tail used as a rudder; long limber legs; a flexible backbone; an expanded nasal cavity for greater air intake; and enlarged arteries, lungs, and heart, the cheetah is an aerodynamic wonder of unparalleled speed. However, because they are built for speed and not for power, cheetahs have trouble competing with larger and more powerful cats that will often steal a cheetah's prey and kill their young. One way cheetahs have dealt with this obstacle is by living outside of game reserves where many of their competitors are found. Consequently, 90 percent of Namibia's cheetahs reside outside of protected areas, alongside humans, many of whom are farmers that see the cheetah as competition for their livestock.

Another unique threat to the future of cheetahs is found even closer to home: in their DNA. Despite their amazing adaptations for speed, cheetahs are in poor shape genetically. When researchers analyzed the cheetah genome in 2016, they discovered a discouraging fact. Of the thirty animal species that had their genomes analyzed at this time, the cheetahs' genome was the least diverse—more like that of inbred domestic cats than wild ones. The fact that all cheetahs are genetically so similar is extremely problematic because genetic diversity within a population is critical to its healthy reproduction, immunity to disease, and adaptation to change. With this lack of genetic diversity and only ten thousand animals left in the wild, Marker believes cheetahs have reached a tipping point. This is the reason she has poured her life into saving this animal. "I don't allow any negativity to stop the course of my work. I can't allow anything to affect my inspiration because the cheetah doesn't have time."

When Marker moved to Namibia, her first task was to sit with farmers and to listen. Livestock farmers, who foremost saw cheetahs as vermin and not as a valuable part of a healthy ecosystem, had killed nearly half of Africa's most endangered big cat, and Marker was all about finding solutions. Most of the farmers wondered why she was so interested in the cheetahs and, equally, in them. "They thought I was strange," she says, "but I sat with them and learned everything I could about their farming systems and wildlife and what they could tell me about the cheetah." Marker understood that in their minds they had valid reasons to shoot cheetahs. "I didn't want to judge. I wanted to try and understand, so we could work together. Still," she notes, "the most difficult part of doing this job is balancing all of the interests of the people involved—the politics of keeping everyone happy. And with cheetahs we will not solve the conservation crisis unless all stakeholders have a voice in the solution."

Keeping everyone happy and giving all stakeholders a voice means caring about livestock farmers (in an arid environment with regular drought, livestock farming is the main form of livelihood) whose decision to pull the trigger could mean one less endangered cat. "You can't ask a farmer to care about conserving wildlife when he's struggling just to feed his family," says Marker. That's why one of CCF's signature programs created by Marker is Future Farmers of Africa, a human-wildlife conflict mitigation initiative. This program works with farmers to find predator-friendly livestock and wildlife management techniques. One such technique Marker pioneered in Namibia in 1994 is the use of Anatolian shepherds and Kangal dogs, physically imposing dogs originally from Turkey, where they have been used for more than five thousand years to guard livestock. The dogs, whom Marker carefully selects, are highly intelligent, protective of the livestock, and able to drive away most large predators. Farmers who have used Anatolian and Kangal dogs to protect their herds have reported drops in predation rates of between 80 and 100 percent—meaning those farmers are less likely to kill or trap cheetahs on their lands. Farmers, in fact, are so enthusiastic about the program that there is a two-year waiting list for puppies. In 2016, Marker's Livestock Guarding Dog program had bred and placed more than five hundred dogs with farmers.

Another innovative brainchild of Marker's is the CCF's Bush Habitat Restoration Project, which produces Bushblok. Bushblok, a low emission, high efficiency fuel log made from processed thornbush, gives farmers an alternative to felling trees for charcoal. Because thornbush is a fast-growing and adaptable plant, it quickly chokes out the cheetah's rangeland habitat and makes cultivation difficult, if not impossible. For Marker's efforts in converting what is essentially a weed into a sustainable and affordable fuel source, she received the Tech Museum's Intel Prize for the Environment in 2008.

The Intel Prize is only one award of the many that she's received. Among other distinguished honors, Marker has won the Tyler Prize for Environmental Achievement in 2010. In 2008, and again in 2010, she was a finalist for the esteemed Indianapolis Prize (a biennial prize awarded by the Indianapolis Zoo to individuals for "extraordinary contributions to conservation efforts affecting one or more animal species"), and in 2000, *Time* magazine named her as a Hero for the Planet—a recognition that, among others, has been given to venerated individuals such as Sylvia Earle and Robert F. Kennedy, Jr.

Marker chalks up the recognition of her conservation work to one key factor: determination. "Determination is the number one thing to be successful at my work. Ask anyone who knows me, I have plenty of that," she says. Still, Marker shares credit with others for her conservation accomplishments. "My work is not a one-woman show. There are thousands of supporters around the globe—staff, volunteers, donors, school kids, wildlife enthusiasts, legislators, and more—all working to protect this species. Supporting and inspiring others is critical if we want our mission to succeed."

With this support and with Marker's vision and innovation, CCF has established a wide range of conservation initiatives from development of predator-friendly products and alternative livelihoods, to model farms and community management conservancies, to outreach and education. Marker has not just changed the face of cheetah conservation in Namibia, she arguably is the face of cheetah conservation. Although there are others working to protect the great cat, Marker is the pioneer of cheetah conservation and the world's leading advocate of their survival. Today, thanks to Marker and her supporters, Namibians are proud to have the designation "Cheetah Capital of the World." "I'm really happy to have precipitated that change with our work," she says.

Outside of her fieldwork, Marker has authored eighty publications and, at age forty-eight, she earned her PhD from Oxford. Her dissertation, *Aspects of Cheetah (Acinonyx jubatus) Biology, Ecology and Conservation Strategies on Namibian Farmlands* (2002) is considered by academics to be the authoritative work on cheetahs.

The programs at CCF are the big pictures of Marker's life. Her day-to-day operations take place at the Cheetah Conservation Fund's Field Research and Education Center, the on-the-ground CCF site she started in 1990 in Otijiwarongo. The Center is home to research facilities, a model farm, an education center and museum, and a sanctuary of resident injured and orphaned cheetahs. Marker's partner, Dr. Bruce Brewer, a conservation scientist, is the general manager of the Center. For Marker, the staff, and the volunteers, a typical day at the Center is taking care of the farm animals (three hundred head of small livestock, goats, and sheep), the livestock guarding dogs (fifteen breeding Anatolian and Kangal dogs and around forty puppies born each year), and the cheetahs (thirty-five orphaned cheetahs), as well as monitoring the various research projects, which include data collection from game counts, camera trapping, and home range data from radio-collared cheetahs. Working to protect the cheetah also means a lot of international communications, data analysis, grant writing, and fundraising—and, as Marker says, "a lot of just plain hard work."

🐾

In order to achieve so much good in the field of conservation, Marker's personal life has taken a back seat. "But, then, what really is a personal life?" she asks. "For me, my life has been about developing a successful conservation organization that helps save cheetahs. Some people may look at my life—with so many demands on my time, endless travel, working on weekends and holidays and every moment I'm able—and call that a personal sacrifice. But honestly? It's an honor to represent the cheetah. It would be a sacrifice not to live each day doing all I can to protect this species, so that they're not just a photo in a book of what used to roam our wild places."

Marker also knows that to protect the cheetah in the long-term, she needs to inspire the next generation—and not just inspire them, but create what she calls a conservation army. And she knows that she can't do it alone.

> Above all, the most important thing we adults can teach our children is to be aware of how our actions and our choices impact the world around us. From a tiny insect or plant, to a magnificent elephant or whale, there are a myriad of living organisms that depend on one another, and ultimately, that depend on us, humans, just as we depend on them. It is our responsibility, as adults, to teach our kids the importance of healthy ecosystems, of maintaining biodiversity.

Healthy ecosystems, biodiversity, and connections to other living creatures are what make Marker happy. While she has had the opportunity to live and connect with both wild and domestic creatures—starting with the horses and goats of her youth, leading to her ten-year relationship with Khayam—she knows that many others have not. She also knows that people don't love what they don't experience or understand, a reason education and exposure to nature are so close to her heart. With this in mind, she and CCF have set out to educate all Namibians about the cheetah, to give them exposure and outreach experiences that will lead to sustainable coexistence with Africa's most endangered cat.

The local people who coexist with cheetahs are the on-the-ground players, the first in line of the conservation of this majestic species. But Marker believes it is not just those living with cheetahs who matter in the fight for their survival. Conservation is a global effort in which all of humanity can, and must, partake. "If we can impress upon today's young people that conservation is everyone's responsibility, we will be ensuring that the next generations become stewards for our planet. However, if we want to leave them a world they can protect, we must work hard to stop today's extinction rates," she says. "If you have just a minute to give, think about our interconnectedness. If you have a day, help spread awareness—a year, plan for changes in the way you live, share with others the needs for change. Each of us has an important role to play. It's just up to us to figure this out and act upon it."

Despite inroads CCF has made into cheetah conservation, Marker is not slowing down. "There is no time to sit back and relax," she says. Although she has made advances in raising public awareness of the problems facing cheetahs, there is still much work to be done, especially in other countries where the cheetah lives, such as Algeria, Angola, Botswana, Kenya, and Niger, and even Iran, with just seventy remaining wild cheetahs. "I have built the model's framework," says Marker, "and the next step is to scale up programs so our strategies can be applied throughout the cheetah's range."

The future and the idea that things can change bring Marker hope. She now seeks to push her conservation efforts even further and to form innovative partnerships, the types of which do not presently exist. "Particularly, we will need to form new partnerships with businesses and investors to work on sustainability, and with government to work on policy. We're moving the needle. And, together, we can continue that movement. Ignite even bigger change still to come."

🐾

Another critical role that Marker and CCF play in cheetah conservation is working to end the illegal pet trade, a multibillion-dollar business with which the cheetah has a long history. Due to their gentler disposition and smaller size in comparison to other big cats such as the lion, cheetahs have historically been a favorite exotic pet for emperors and pharaohs. Even today, people seek to own this animal as a status symbol. Because cheetahs are so difficult to breed in captivity, most of the people who own them have obtained them illegally—meaning the cheetah is taken from the wild, and in many cases, the mother is killed so the cubs can be sold. According to Marker, only one in six cubs actually survives to the point of sale, usually in the Middle East. To make matters worse, the illegal trade is happening in those countries with a tiny cheetah population, so the loss of even one animal is devastating.

Marker and CCF got involved in the illegal pet trade in 2005 after they received a call from a US Marine who needed help rescuing two cheetah cubs tied outside of a restaurant in Ethiopia. With CCF's help, the cubs were rescued, but the two young animals eventually died. With characteristic optimism and hope, Marker believes the cubs' lives have not been in vain, as international attention was brought towards the issue and towards combating what she calls "this devastating crime against conservation." Since that call in 2005, CCF has taken an internationally leading role in the fight against the illegal pet trade in cheetahs.

While much of her work involves interacting and negotiating with humans, fortunately, Marker has been able to balance her human time with cheetah time. "One of the most rewarding aspects of my work has been being able to learn about cheetahs in the wild, observing them and tracking their movements, today using satellite collars," she says. One such cheetah Marker and the CCF team has observed and tracked is Zinzi, an orphaned cub Marker blogged about on CCF's website.

Starting in 2009 when a farmer brought her to CCF, having found her orphaned and alone, Zinzi spent nearly three years at CCF's Bellebeno cheetah camp, a two-hundred-acre sanctuary. With limited human contact and solid care, Zinzi was eventually released into the wild. Once released, CCF monitored her to make sure she was surviving and entirely self-sufficient. Good news came on September 12, 2015: Zinzi wasn't just surviving, she was thriving. Based on information from Zinzi's radio collar, it appeared she had had cubs, and in November of that year, the CCF monitoring team spotted her four cubs for the first time. Zinzi's success was Marker's success. With every cheetah that survives, that is rescued, that isn't shot, and that is put back into the wild, Marker has cause to celebrate. Her victories come one cheetah at a time.

Marker is aware of all the ups and downs that come with working with a species on the brink, and, as such, she is a paradox; both a determined optimist and a practical realist. "If humans don't act quickly to make big changes now, in a few years there will not be enough cheetahs remaining in the wild to save the species from extinction," she says with a plea to the world community. "What a horrible thought. Please don't let that happen. Humans aren't going away anytime soon, and if we don't learn to live with wildlife, we will end up without them and that would be a horrible place to be."

She offers the following advice to those people who want to help: "Keep it honest, keep your mission pure and the right things will happen, whether or not you think they are right at the time. Understand that the path to succeeding in our mission does not have a straight line. Be patient and remain focused. Look for practical solutions and don't give up. Conservation takes a long time."

Conservation takes a long time, but for cheetahs, time is just what they don't have. Humanity must act fast if we are to save the fastest animal on earth. Good thing Laurie Marker and her thousands of dedicated volunteers and supporters are at their side.

For more information on Laurie Marker, visit www.cheetah.org.

CHAPTER 6

• • •

Dr. Kushal Konwar Sarma, PhD: The Man Who Speaks for Asian Elephants

"It is up to man, the elephant's friend throughout the ages, to take decisive steps to ensure its preservation."

—Dr. Kushal Konwar Sarma

Credit: Lisa Mills

Dr. Kushal Konwar Sarma.

EARLY ON A JANUARY MORNING in 2015, a young bull elephant stepped on a sagging power line in the Paneri Tea Plantation in the Udalgari district of Assam, India. The elephant's soft-padded feet conducted the current, and the animal fell, kicking in the mud. The local veterinarian called to the scene thought the tusker (not all male Asian elephants have tusks; those that do are called tuskers) was going to die. The forest department warden didn't agree. With proper treatment, he believed the animal could survive. He called the one person who could help: Dr. Kushal Konwar Sarma (KK to those who know him well), India's beloved elephant doctor.

Dr. Sarma received the call at 6 a.m. Although he was several hours away in Guwahati, the state capital, he didn't hesitate. He packed his supplies and headed into the field. "With elephants," says Dr. Sarma, "I never get tired."

🐾

With more than eight hundred large tea estates and thousands of smaller tea gardens yielding more than seven hundred million pounds of black tea annually, Assam is the most productive tea-producing region in the world. The state is also home to more than 10 percent of the world's remaining Asian elephants. With an explosive human population and hardly any habitat available for a mega herbivore that requires six hundred pounds of food and one hundred gallons of water each day, the elephants of the region tend to congregate in what space is available: tea plantations. Unfortunately, tea and elephants don't mix. "Tea plantations are death traps for elephants," says Dr. Sarma. "There's not a blade of grass for them to eat. There are pesticides on the leaves, weedicides on the ground, and little or nothing for them to drink—and if there is any water, it is highly contaminated with harmful chemicals. There are trenches elephant calves often fall into and sagging electric lines."

🐾

By the time Dr. Sarma arrived in Paneri, some two thousand people were gathered. To add to the pressure of the human audience already on hand, a herd of elephants was watching from a distance. Relying on his years of experience treating both wild and captive elephants, Dr. Sarma went to work. "The problem was the elephant was kicking and rolling, so I couldn't get close. I fixed some wooden poles behind his head, so he couldn't keep turning. Then I held his ear and exposed the veins to give the medicine," he explains. "I injected a cocktail of drugs intended to help with the kidney damage and abnormal acid in the blood caused by severe electrocution."

After Dr. Sarma gave the medicine, the elephant lifted his head and sniffed the air with his trunk, signs that he was more comfortable. "The real problem, however, had just begun," recalls Dr. Sarma. "How was I going to get an elephant that was weak, dehydrated, and exhausted to his feet? I decided to find a local forklift driver and ask for his help." Now there was a new problem to cope with: a bull elephant can easily crush a truck, not to mention a person. The forklift driver, well aware of this fact, was not eager to oblige. "He told me it was too dangerous," says Dr. Sarma. "I told him, 'you only die once,' and I climbed into the cab."

Seeing how brave the doctor was, the driver sighed and climbed in after him. With considerable effort and delicate maneuvering, the two men were able to slowly raise the tusker to his feet. Once up, the elephant glanced in Dr. Sarma's direction, then turned and wandered off. "This glance," Dr. Sarma says, "was all the payment I needed."

That particular tusker is just one of many elephants that Dr. Sarma has helped during his nearly thirty years as a veterinarian. During his long career, he has saved and treated thousands of elephants, and he holds the world's record for restraining dangerous rogues (solitary elephants—usually males—that become dangerous and unpredictably violent) that would likely be killed, or kill, if not for him.

🐾

Dr. Sarma's love of elephants began as a child. As one of six children, he grew up in a family compound with twenty-five extended family members in a village called Barama, located in the Kamrup district of Assam. His childhood elephant (there is a long history of captive elephants in India), an old female named Lakshmi (named for the goddess of wealth in the Hindu faith) lived in the orchard attached to his family's home. He recalls how each morning the *mahout* (handler) bathed Lakshmi in the *Mora-pagladia*, a clear, blue river that begins in the hills of Bhutan and flows through Barama. The *mahout* would then lead Lakshmi back to the orchard where she'd eagerly await the arrival of Dr. Sarma's grandmother, a small woman who often dressed in a white *Mekhela Chador*, a typical two-piece outfit worn by Assamese women. "Elephants are highly expressive creatures, capable of feeling deep emotion and of showing their feelings," says Dr. Sarma. Lakshmi's squeaks and restless behavior made it clear that she wanted to see her friend.

"I would beg the *mahout* to let me sit on the elephant and be with her as she grazed," Dr. Sarma says. "Often the *mahout* obliged, and

I spent the afternoon on Lakshmi's back as she went to the orchard and fed on bamboo and pina grass growing alongside the river. My mother would scold me when I came home dirty, covered in insect bites, my legs chafed and scratched. I was a respectful child and her reproach bothered me—but not enough to stop me. The next day I'd be out riding Lakshmi." Aside from riding Lakshmi, Dr. Sarma worked hard and got excellent grades. When he was old enough, he left his village and attended college and then veterinary school. He became a vet in 1983 and after obtaining a master's degree in veterinary surgery in 1986, joined the vet school in Assam as faculty. In 1994, he earned a PhD in veterinary surgery, with a specialty in anesthesiology. The degree, it turns out, would come in handy in a way he never expected.

🐾

Elephants have an important role and a complex history in India, where they are revered as the incarnation of the elephant-headed god Lord Ganesha in the Hindu religion. Aside from the approximately five thousand to six thousand wild elephants in Assam, and ten thousand in the region, there are an additional one thousand two hundred captive ones. Not only does Dr. Sarma look after and care for the majority of these captive elephants, but he often risks his life to save them—and to save villagers. One of the main reasons Dr. Sarma is called on to save a captive elephant has to do with a condition called *musth*.

Musth, from the Hindi word meaning "intoxicated," is a natural state that happens each year when a healthy bull elephant in his twenties or older gets a surge of testosterone that increases his sexual appetite and makes him challenge other bulls for females. An elephant in *musth* may have as much as fifty times his normal testosterone level and the condition can last from several weeks to several months. With so many people, so many elephants, and so little space, if a *musth* bull escapes his *mahout* he might displace his aggression and kill someone; this, in turn, may lead the government to declare him a rogue and put out the order to have him killed.

Until 1994, there was no procedure for how to recapture a rogue *musth* bull in Assam, and no recognized practice for how to sedate an injured wild elephant in need of surgery or care. On a December day, deep in the forests of Arunachal Pradesh, a neighboring state of Assam, Dr. Sarma used what he had learned while earning his PhD, and in doing so made elephant history. "A man named Rajesh came to my office. He explained he had come because his elephant, Manik, had gone into *musth* and escaped his *mahout*," Dr. Sarma says. "Manik had smashed two logging trucks. Villagers feared his rampage would get worse." Rajesh had heard about Dr. Sarma's PhD. He had seen a video and learned that it might be possible for aggressive wild animals to be restrained from a distance using a dart laced with a sleep-inducing drug.

Rajesh pleaded with Dr. Sarma to travel one hundred and twenty miles to Tipi, his village in Arunachal Pradesh, and to try this technique on Manik. He went on to say that the tribal councilor had given orders for Manik to be killed in twenty-four hours if he couldn't be restrained. Hunters had already arrived and were stationed in the forested hills around Tipi where the elephant had last been seen. "He was telling me that I was Manik's only chance," says Dr. Sarma. "I contemplated what was being asked of me. Chemically restraining a dangerous animal could get me killed. Nobody had ever used this technique here before. I was being asked to practice something new and to succeed on the first try." Going head-to-head with his hesitation was his desire to save Manik. "I realized if I said no, there'd be no way out for Manik but death."

Dr. Sarma ultimately agreed to help. He obtained a rusty syringe projector from the Assam State Zoo ("A device that looked more like a gun than a tool to save an elephant"), two metal syringe barrels, feathered flight directors, rubber plungers, syringe charges for five ml darts, and long-range cartridges. Then he set out.

On the first night of the two-day journey Dr. Sarma was kept awake first by worry, then by mosquitoes, then by a whole *biraderi* (community) of mice. "I applied the *pashupat* (the strongest weapon of God) mimicking a cat's meow," he says. The ploy worked and the mice left, but only to be replaced by the steam engine and the roosters. At first light, after a sleepless night, it was time to continue the trip. The road to Tipi snaked up through the Himalayan foothills, a road, opposed to many in India that are cratered with potholes, that Dr. Sarma calls "a traveler's delight." At 10:30 a.m., Dr. Sarma reached Tipi. He was not happy about what he found there. "There was a Nepalese forester, two rowdy-looking tribal hunters, and two majestic-looking Magnum rifles lying by their sides," he says. "They looked at me with contempt. They were probably assured of their own success in killing Manik and the booty from the government for eliminating the rogue, plus an extra reward in the form of the elephant's ivory."

Dr. Sarma did not have much time. He again set out, this time along rough roads littered with boulders that took half an hour to drive a single mile. He then hired a young man named Phuleswar to come with him and to fire the syringe, and the two hiked to the spot where Manik had last been seen. "I must confess having felt nervous while preparing the tranquilizing gun," says Dr. Sarma. "I handed the gun over to Phuleswar and detailed him on its use."

When Dr. Sarma finally spotted Manik, he took cover behind a boulder and Phuleswar climbed into a tree from where he could best hit his target. "Manik, with his head raised and ears erect, galloped furiously to the tree where Phuleswar was perched. The elephant roared twice while charging ahead, and I feared that if he hit the tree where Phuleswar was sitting he'd be killed," says Dr. Sarma. Realizing the threat, Phuleswar threw a handful of *bheem kal* fruits, a variety of sweet banana, to Manik. The lure of a favorite treat stopped the charging tusker, and Phuleswar fired the syringe and hit his target.

"I rushed down as fast as possible, crossing the rocky bridge, and watched the standing giant barely one hundred feet away. His eyes were closed and he was snoring," says Dr. Sarma. Manik had been sedated, and Dr. Sarma could now recapture the tusker and save him from the hunter's gun.

On that day in 1994, Dr. Sarma made history. What he essentially did in Arunachal Pradesh as a field experiment is now a mainstay in wildlife management practices. As of 2016, Dr. Sarma has rescued and helped 138 rogues.

Restraining and treating aggressive elephants is a physically demanding task, but at age fifty-seven, Dr. Sarma shows no signs of slowing down. With his deep brown eyes, thick mustache, and baseball cap, there is youthfulness to the elephant doctor, who says that in his thirty-year career he has never taken off a weekend. Weekend highlights have included getting defecated on by an elephant to whom he was giving an enema, being covered in leeches as he hiked through forests to track a rogue, and, more than once, nearly getting killed—all to save elephants, jobs for which he does not get paid, or at best, gets paid a token sum. While he could make a lot more money working full time with dogs and cats in an air-conditioned office, it is not money that motivates him.

"I am a field type of man," he states simply. "What elephants have done for me I could not repay in ten lifetimes. My heart is with the forest, with the land, with the people, and most of all, with the elephants, the last of the greatest creatures on earth. Without the elephants, I am nobody."

In addition to fieldwork and responsibilities at Assam Agricultural University in Guwahati where he is head of the Department of Surgery and Radiology in the College of Veterinary Science, Dr. Sarma has written four books used throughout Asia in elephant care, written over 135 research papers and clinical reports and over fifty popular and scientific papers, organized two national-level trainings on elephants for university teachers, and runs free elephant health-care clinics throughout Assam.

Despite all of his achievements, Dr. Sarma is not boastful. He has hardly any social media presence. He does not care about fame or self-promotion. He cares simply about elephants, about the people of India, and about saving forests. To lead the kind of life he does, Dr. Sarma says, "You need to have a love of animals, whether or not you earn a lot of money. You also need a desire to help and to take up the task, even if it means driving long distances. You have to have a sense of adventure and be ready to go. Give me five minutes and I'm ready. I don't waste a minute when it comes to helping animals." When he gets called to treat an animal, even if he's busy, he says, "I just put other issues aside."

Dr. Sarma sidelines these other concerns because he cares deeply about animals and about conservation. Yet, in a nation the size of India with over one billion people, many of whom are marginalized and cutting down the forest for survival, conservation isn't easy. "Where there is space in India, it gets filled," he explains. "The governments of India and of third-world countries need to adopt policies to stabilize the burgeoning populations."

Although deforestation and population growth go hand in hand, what Dr. Sarma would like most is for the remaining forests to be left untouched. "One should not just think of the forests as a source of livelihood, be it collecting fodder for animals, firewood for our kitchen fire or fireplace, and clearing the forest for cultivation and settlement," he says. "We must think about the value of forests for our source of oxygen and water and for the very survival of all species on earth, and we must educate young people."

Education about elephants and conservation is especially important in the Udalgari district of Assam, which is thought to have the highest rate of human-elephant conflict in the world. In this densely populated area, desperate and hungry elephants trample homes, raid rice paddy fields, and sometimes a stressed animal kills a person. For the elephants, the situation is no easier. They face an obstacle course of threats, including poisoning by pesticides, trenches, electrocution, and an overall loss of habitat. Dr. Sarma works in Udalgari with a grassroots nonprofit called Elephants on the Line (EOL). The foundation's aim is to mitigate human-elephant conflict and restore habitat for elephants. Dr. Sarma's role in the project is fundamental to its success. He has developed an educational outreach of "do's and dont's" of living with elephants that has been translated into Assamese, Bodo, and Hindi—the three main languages of the district. He has also trained a cadre of local young men from the district about elephant behavior, ecology, and habitat requirements. These young men are the on-the-ground team who take what they've learned and share the information with hundreds of school children and villagers throughout Udalgari.

While all animals inspire Dr. Sarma (such as the one-horned rhinoceros, an animal he is helping bring back from the brink of extinction), elephants are his main love. He never feels hopeless, but he worries about what will happen to his beloved friends and where they will go as human population grows. "We are a civilized people. If we don't do anything, it's a shame on us," he says. "We have to minimize our greediness, our 'I need' mentality." His vision of the future is nothing short of demanding: "I require a future in which we as humanity find our best selves and protect the last of the greatest creatures on earth. If we destroy the forests, we are doomed. Nature must be protected or else we go down with the elephants."

Fortunately, Dr. Sarma has passed down his intelligence, his passion, and his dedication to his daughter, Nina, who is receiving a bachelor's degree in veterinary science at Assam Agricultural University in 2016, and hopes to be an elephant doctor like her father. "After all," Dr. Sarma says, "it's up to the next generation to continue our work."

As India's leading elephant doctor, Dr. Sarma attends many international conferences on elephant health care and conservation. When it is his turn to introduce himself and say who he works for, he doesn't say he works for a university or a nonprofit. Dr. Sarma simply tells the conference attendees that he represents the elephants.

For more information on Dr. Sarma, please visit www.elephantdoctor.in.

CHAPTER 7

• • •

Paul Hilton: Investigative Photojournalist of the Illegal Wildlife Trade

"Once you've seen the truth you can't just leave it and not actually try to expose it and inform people about other species that can't stand up for themselves."

—Paul Hilton

Credit: Shawn Heinrichs

Paul Hilton.

S UMATRAN ORANGUTANS, ASIATIC BLACK BEARS, whale sharks, manta rays—Hong Kong–based conservation photojournalist Paul Hilton photographs them all. His pictures capture the soul and the suffering of his subjects: animals caught in the illegal wildlife trade and those trying to survive in some of the most critically endangered habitats on earth.

Hilton, who has loved animals since he was a small child, is unafraid to look at the grim reality of the often brutal relationship between humans and the rest of the natural world. His photos force you to look; they beg you to stop and think. As a photographer, Hilton has one main goal: "I want people to view my images and understand what's really going on out there."

🐾

As a young boy growing up first in Lancashire, England, then in northeastern Australia, Hilton loved animals. "My grandfather had a farm and my mom would always take me down there," he says. "She later told me that I'd be really good and quiet when I was with the animals, but as soon as she took me away from the barn, I would cry and have a tantrum." When he was about two years old, his mother started working part time in a pet store, and it was the best possible babysitter for her animal-loving son. As his mother worked, she would move Paul around the shop, placing him in front of fish tanks and birdcages. She didn't have to worry about him. He'd sit content for hours, checking out the various creatures. At home, there were animals, too. "I had magpies, cockatoos, galahs, ducks, chickens, snakes, even a donkey," says Hilton. Once a mother fruit bat (a furry bat with a fox-like face that dwells primarily in trees and eats fruit—different from the insect-eating microbats) was electrocuted outside of his house and a baby fell off the mother's back. "We didn't know they carried viruses at the time, so it ended up living in my cupboard. I nicknamed him Moonshine. We fed him and he lived with us until one day we put him outside and he flew off into the wild."

When he finished high school, Hilton thought about working for the Queensland Parks and Wildlife Services, but he realized that would mean spending all his time in the remote Australian Outback at such a young age. He then thought about pursuing photography, but his family said it wasn't a viable career and told him to stop dreaming. But Hilton was a dreamer—the world was vast and he wanted to see it. Because he wasn't ready for college, he decided to "go on a walkabout for a year" and took off in an Australian Kombi campervan to see the country. Instead of a pet shop, this time a van became Hilton's personal menagerie. Because Hilton couldn't pass an injured animal without wanting to help it, the back of the Kombi became home to hurt blue-tongued lizards, water pythons, and cockatoos. "Eventually," he says, "I let them all go."

Although his family had previously protested the idea of Hilton becoming a photographer, after his van trip, he decided to go to London to take a course in basic photography at a studio in Kennington. On a stop in Hong Kong on the way back to Australia once the course finished, he met Michel Porro, a freelance Dutch photographer. Hilton was twenty years old at the time, and when Porro offered him a job shooting portraits, weddings, and homes, he tried it out. The job wasn't the right fit for a young man whose passion was animals and the outdoors, so he started doing pro bono photographic work for Hong Kong environmental and wildlife groups, such as World Wildlife Fund. Then, in 2000, he met Jill Robinson of the Animals Asia Foundation (AAF) and he got his first break.

AAF was working to stop bear bile farming in China. The bile, which is extracted from the bears under horrific circumstances, is sold in some Traditional Chinese Medicine (TCM) treatments and also for non-medicinal products such as shampoos, hemorrhoid creams, and herbal teas. AAF was about to rescue the first bear ever from a bear bile farm, and Robinson asked Hilton to come along and photograph the event. Hilton explains:

> The bears were brought in from a farm in these tiny crusher cages that their bodies had grown into. Some of them had spent more than a decade in these conditions. We pulled out ten or fifteen bears from the cages, and I documented the whole thing. There was one bear, Andrew, who had lost a leg to a snare. He was the first bear AAF rescued and operated on to pull out a six-inch steel catheter from his gall bladder. He was so friendly and well natured and lived as the AAF mascot for a few years afterwards. A lot of the other bears were angry and mentally unstable and full of cancer in their bodies from all the stress. Many died.

For Hilton's photos—which were featured in *Asia Geographic* in 2001 and captured everything from the crusher cages in which the bears are kept, to the emotion of the people working to save them, to the bears themselves—he won the Ark Trust Award in an event hosted by the Humane Society. *National Geographic* later ran a piece with one of his photographs. "I thought, okay, well, maybe there is an angle here for me," says Hilton. "Maybe I can do more of this."

It was not immediately evident how to find more similar work, but another grim animal trend unfortunately was clear: harvesting shark fins. It was everywhere in Hong Kong, and Hilton was enraged by what he was seeing. "I was sick to death of walking by shop fronts with crazy amounts of sharks' fins piled on top of each other for sale. Something was wrong, but it seemed to be acceptable to everyone else." He decided he would go and do something about it. He didn't have the support or backing of an organization. This he'd do on his own. "I wanted to paint a picture of what was going on and what people were supporting when they sat down to eat a bowl of shark fin soup. People in Hong Kong had no idea at the time. Even the World Wildlife Fund didn't know how serious the issue was."

Doing it on his own meant putting himself in dangerous, if not life-threatening, situations as he boarded long-liner fishing boats upon which massive numbers of sharks were being slaughtered, or ventured into facilities that were processing the fins. He recalls one occasion when he entered a shark fin processing plant. "People began shouting at me to get out. As I started backing out a guy started hitting me in the back of the legs with a crowbar." Hilton didn't think about the pain. He thought about protecting the camera with his documentation on what was happening.

Although he doesn't like confrontation, when he enters a potentially charged situation, Hilton says, "I think, okay, if I don't do this, who else is going to?" In order to gain access to places where photographers may not be welcome, he says, "When you board a boat or enter a processing facility, it's like acting. I can sit there like I'm somebody else. It's all about confident body language. They can read you and you have to be able to read people." Being nosy helps, too. "I have a curious mind and I stick my nose in places it sometimes shouldn't be." He also adds that it's easier to ask for forgiveness than to ask for permission.

Due in large part to his confidence and courage, Hilton's photos became the catalyst for the anti–shark fin movement in Hong Kong. He continued photographing the brutal industry for Greenpeace

International, and in 2012 was awarded a World Press Photo Award for his body of work on the issue. (The World Press Photo Award is one of the most prestigious awards in photojournalism and multimedia story-telling. Approximately four million people worldwide see the exhibition it produces each year.) He also wrote a book, *Man and Shark* (2010), the first bilingual book on the subject (written in Chinese and English) that traces a fin from the shark to the person who eats it. Hilton wants consumers to look closely at their choices and see how their everyday decisions affect apex predators that have been around for 400 million years and whose populations are now threatened across species.

While investigating the shark fin industry, another disturbing trend caught Hilton's attention: the large-scale killing of manta and mobula rays. These graceful creatures of tropical and subtropical waters were being slain for their gill rakers—the bony processes of the gill arch that help filter feeders trap small prey. Like shark fins, gill rakers are sold for use in TCM, with 99 percent of the market in Guangzhou in Southern China. Biologists know little about manta rays; however, they do know that mantas have the largest brain of any fish, that they are the largest of all the rays (a manta ray can be twenty-nine feet and weigh up to three thousand pounds), and that they are slow to mature and to reproduce, giving birth to one or two pups every two to five years. Due to their slow reproduction, mantas are vulnerable to overfishing.

Hilton's photos helped to expose the assault against manta rays, but he wanted to do more than just photograph what he was seeing. He wanted to be directly involved in the action. "Besides taking a photo and shining a light on an issue, I wanted to help create campaigns," Hilton says. In 2009, in order to be more involved with the manta ray crisis, he helped set up the Manta Ray of Hope project, a collaboration of nonprofit organizations, researchers, dive operators, governments, and local communities, to save mantas and mobulas from this unsustainable trade. In 2013 he was also instrumental in getting manta rays listed under CITES (the Convention on International Trade in Endangered Species of Wild Fauna and Flora) Appendix II, a designation for species that are not immediately threatened with extinction but that may become so unless trade is closely controlled.

Although he is still concerned about sharks and rays and hasn't turned his back on the ocean ("there was a 50 percent decline in shark fin consumption after our campaign, though I think it is going up again, so I have to put more energy back into that soon"), Hilton's current focus is on Indonesia's Leuser Ecosytem, a forested mountain area in northern Sumatra. Home to the Sumatran elephant, rhinoceros, tiger, orangutan, as well as the clouded leopard, sun bear, loris, and many other species, this six-and-a-half million–acre ecosystem is one of the most biologically rich regions of rainforest in Southeast Asia—and one of the most threatened.

Like so many other vulnerable and biologically diverse ecosystems across the world, pristine forest land in Indonesia is being destroyed at an alarming rate—burned, felled, and cleared—in this case for palm oil, an ingredient pervasive in a variety of snack foods from peanut butter to cookies, and in products as diverse as shampoos, detergents, soaps, and candles. In fact, palm oil is the most widely used oil in the world. After flying into Sumatra on assignment for a local grassroots NGO and seeing the destruction for the first time in 2012, Hilton says, "It's like someone had given the land a bad haircut."

When it comes to Leuser, Hilton believes that, as consumers, we are very powerful. "The choices we make on a daily basis have a huge impact across the world," he says. The palm oil situation can be a conundrum for concerned consumers, as boycotting the product will lead to cultivation of other oils that take more land to be grown. Hilton suggests people try to buy certified sustainable palm oil products (CSPO), so as not to become unwitting accomplices in the destruction of Indonesia's forests for a snack.

Hilton was glad to have a little star power to bring attention to this issue when in March 2016 Oscar-winning actors Adrien Brody and Leonardo DiCaprio visited Leuser National Park to call attention to the crisis. On Instagram, DiCaprio posted the message: "The Leonardo DiCaprio Foundation is supporting local partners to establish a megafauna sanctuary in the Leuser Ecosystem, the last place on earth where Sumatran orangutans, tigers, rhinos, and elephants coexist in the wild."

One animal Hilton has focused on in his attempt to shed light on the Indonesian situation is the Sumatra orangutan. With only fourteen thousand of these animals left, Hilton says, "It is now or never for those of us who are trying to save the Sumatran orangutan, as the last of its natural habitats come under threat from chainsaws."

It is not just chainsaws, though, that are killing the Sumatran orangutan; it is the illegal wildlife trade. To expose the issue, Hilton again put himself at risk. In 2012, posing as a tourist interested in buying a pet orangutan, he was able to photograph the grueling conditions under which one animal was being kept and, in doing so, eventually secure its release.

Being involved in so many hard issues can be "soul destroying," and some images stay with Hilton, such as a series of photographs he took on an assignment to document the pangolin trade. (Pangolins are scaly burrowing animals that eat ants and termites and are one of the most endangered mammal groups in the world.) In April 2015, he wrote a piece for the *National Geographic Voices* blog called "Pangolin Prison," for which he received an award in 2016 at the National History Museum in London. The feature covered an investigation by the Wildlife Conservation Society's Wildlife Crimes Unit of the illegal trade of pangolins in Medan, Sumatra. "I can't shake the photo," he says of one specific image he captured of thousands of dead and frozen pangolins that had come from the area bordering the Leuser Ecosystem and were headed to Southern China for the exotic meat trade and TCM. Thanks in large part to Hilton's work, the trader was arrested. About his important contributions, Hilton remarks:

> It's heavy work, and I see a lot of animals suffering and a lot of forests being bulldozed down. I look back over the years and think, *wow, there's been a lot of carnage out there.* There are times I lose hope in humanity. Other times I feel hopeful. There's still so much worth fighting for and so much beauty out there. I can go to the forest and see orangutans or elephants or go to the ocean and see manta rays, schools of hammerhead sharks, or whales.

As a man who loves all animals equally and who spends the majority of his time with wild creatures, Hilton has had many memorable meetings with his subjects. One encounter he recalls happened with an elephant. In 2014, Hilton was trying to get a photograph for a campaign on wild Sumatran elephants and the ivory trade. He found a guide to show him where the elephants were, but the guide was nervous, advising Hilton to be careful because elephants were dangerous. Then they saw an elephant trunk sticking out from the trees. "That's it, the guide freaks out and leaves," says Hilton. "So I sit down next to the river because I know elephants have bad eyesight, and I'm downwind so it won't smell me."

As Hilton sat there, first a bull elephant came out from the trees, and then elephants of all ages started to appear. "The bull elephant greeted each one that came out," recalls Hilton. "I was maybe fifty feet away for about twenty minutes. Obviously the bull was telling the other elephants it was safe. I realized how sensitive, emotional, and thoughtful they are."

These intimate moments with other species are what keep Hilton going, what allow him to stay for long periods of time in sterile hotel rooms, to be away from his wife and two daughters, and to put his life at risk. When he does have a victory, however small, he says, "It's important to take time and take it in because that is what you are working for."

He also teaches his children, and those closer to his home in Indonesia, to care about other creatures. If someone is being cruel to an animal, he will try to stop them, reaching out and taking it to a personal level. "Recently I confiscated a water monitor that some people were trying to sell for its skin," he says. "I was with my kids and I told a small lie, saying I was with the Bali Zoo and I was taking the monitor there. I was wearing a shirt that looked official, so the people believed me. We took the monitor and released it into the forest." Maybe it was just one animal that he helped, but helping a single creature exemplifies Hilton's favorite quote by philosopher Edmund Burke: "No one could make a greater mistake than he who did nothing because he could only do a little."

For his efforts on a larger scale, Hilton has received many accolades. Besides the awards for his photographs on bear bile farming and the shark fin industry, Hilton received an award in *Asia Geographic Best of the Decade* series for his work between 1999 and 2009. In 2009, he joined the ranks of renowned conservationists such as Thomas Mangelsen, Wade Davis, and Beverly Joubert to become a member of the International League of Conservation Photographers, whose mission is to further environmental and cultural conservation through ethical photography. In 2012, and again in 2014, he was awarded Wildlife Photographer of the Year by the Natural History Museum in London, and in 2016 the same museum awarded him Wildlife Photojournalist of the Year. His undercover footage of the illegal wildlife trade featured heavily in the 2015 film *Racing Extinction*. His photographs have been published in the *New York Times*, the *International Herald*, *Newsweek*, and *Time*, and he has collaborated with organizations such as WildAid, Rainforest Action Network, Wildlife Conservation Society, Humane Society International, Greenpeace International, and the Hong Kong Shark Foundation.

Despite the honors and successes, Hilton still wonders about the impact of his work. "It's hard to actually put value or merit on what I do," he says. "There's no way of recording it." He hopes, though, that his photos will help people understand the connection to and importance of all species. "People don't always understand the value other species and ecosystems bring to the planet. People say, 'well, if we lose a pangolin or elephant, it doesn't affect me.' As these resources dwindle and the human population increases, everyone will be forced to understand how we need to coexist with these species and ecosystems and how the future of the planet depends on it." He is still hopeful that this change in consciousness will happen. "I think there will be an acceleration that will happen quickly." He then adds, "Because it has to."

It's said that a picture says a thousand words, and Hilton's pictures truly speak those words for those who can't speak for themselves.

For more information on Paul Hilton and examples of his photography, please visit www.instagram.com/paulhiltonphoto.

CHAPTER 8

...

Steven Amstrup, PhD: Saving the World One Polar Bear at a Time

"Polar bear conservation can't be done in the Arctic. It's done down here where you and I live. And it can only be accomplished by changing the way we live."

—Dr. Steven C. Amstrup

Steven Amstrup.

IN EARLY 2000, AS PART of a study to identify polar bear maternal denning habitat, Dr. Steve Amstrup was measuring the sizes, shapes, and snow cover over the top of polar bear dens on Alaska's North Slope. Amstrup was certain the female occupying the den he wanted to measure had departed, but as he was removing the drifted snow over what he thought was the den exit, his right foot plunged into the lair. The surprise of falling through the roof of the den was followed by an even bigger surprise: the den was not empty. There, only inches from his thigh, was a female polar bear. Though Amstrup had been up close to hundreds of polar bears, and he is not one to anthropomorphize, he felt an emotional connection with that animal. "She could've bit me, pulled me into the den, and killed me," he says. "But she didn't. Our eyes connected momentarily, and I swear to God, she had what I would call a perplexed and sad look, like 'What's going on here, what does this mean?' It was almost as if she knew I was there to help her."

The look lasted mere seconds before the two resumed their natural roles of researcher and predator. Unable to stand, Amstrup rolled down hill, pulling his leg from the lair. The mother bear burst out of the den and came after him, but apparently realizing he wasn't a threat, she turned toward Amstrup's colleague, Geoff York, who, when backing away, also fell down. "She could've easily had him, but she didn't," says Amstrup. "Once he fell down, she wasn't interested in him either." When the helicopter pilot who'd brought them there figured out what was happening and started the engine, the bear ran off, giving the two researchers a chance to regroup and then to quickly and carefully take their measurements of the now empty den.

It was then they had their third surprise: two cubs were in the den. "We gathered those cubs and ear-tagged them," says Amstrup. "Then we flew out and caught the mother bear. We ear-tagged her and put her in a net so we could carry her back to the den where they all would be together when the effects of the immobilizing drug wore off." Because the cubs were not radio-collared, Amstrup was unable to track their progress, and he didn't know their fate during the ensuing years. But in the spring of 2016, he got a call from another colleague, George Durner, who was working in the same area. Durner told Amstrup that he had captured one of those cubs from sixteen years ago. The bear was now a big, healthy male, weighing more than one thousand pounds. "A recapture makes you feel good," Amstrup says, "especially when it's an animal that was originally captured as a cub. When they're cubs, they're small and vulnerable, and we know that only about half of the cubs that are born survive to adulthood. Even those that do survive, like this one, often are not recaptured for some time."

Although falling into a polar bear den with cubs could have proven dangerous—if not fatal—Amstrup, who has been studying *Ursus maritimus* on the North Slope of Alaska near the Beaufort Sea for over thirty years, says the real risk of working in the Arctic isn't the bears. The real risk is flying in small aircraft in bad weather to remote areas where help is far away. With his long-term studies and close-up observations of polar bear habitat, including the occasional night with sea ice as a pillow ("For the most part it's like winter camping, except the substrate is moving and you hear the creaking and grinding of the ice."), Amstrup intimately knows what is happening in the Arctic. He has seen the changes to sea ice brought on by climate change, and as such, these days his attention is on education and outreach about the effects of global warming.

His message: It's not too late to save this iconic species. But we have to act now.

Amstrup was born in Fargo, North Dakota, in 1950 and first became interested in all bears as a child. "It was the special nature of these really big carnivores that made a living out there in the woods or on the pack ice that captured my imagination," he says. As far back as he remembers, his goal was to try to preserve landscapes and habitats. He understood that bears, as large carnivores, require healthy and diverse habitats and management of human causes of mortality, and that awareness is what set him on a life mission of conservation. "If we can save an environment that supports bears, it can also support a lot of other things."

He attended college at the University of Washington (UW) where he received a bachelor's degree in forestry in 1972. At that time UW didn't have an official "wildlife management" degree, but the college of forestry offered a major in wildlife, and that was the direction he took. The years he was working on his BS degree were also the years when people were getting serious about studying bears, grizzlies in particular. Black bears, however, despite their wide range and broad distribution across North America, had not yet been the subject of many serious studies. "One of the things that attracted me to black bears was the dearth of information about them. I guess I thought if I could find a good program to study them, there would be great opportunity to make a conservation contribution."

Amstrup's timing was good. In 1972 he entered a master's program in wildlife management at the University of Idaho. There, his major professor, Morris Hornocker, was just starting a black bear study in conjunction with the Idaho Department of Fish and Game. Amstrup's work on that project was the first comprehensive study to use radio tracking to understand movements and habitat use of black bears in the West. In so doing, Amstrup found out something new about these animals: Whereas researchers previously thought that all black bear behavior was the same regardless of where they were found, Amstrup discovered that this was not true. "Black bears, like many other animals, have different behaviors in different portions of their geographic range," he says. In his study area, for example, black bears didn't defend their territories, but had extensively overlapping home ranges. In other geographic regions, they could be much more territorial.

Amstrup earned his master's degree in 1975. Even though he knew he'd eventually obtain a PhD, he first wanted to work and get more field experience. After a stint in Utah as a regional game biologist doing things like trapping and transplanting sheep and sage grouse, he moved to a position in Wyoming with the United States Fish and Wildlife Service (USFW). There he studied pronghorn antelope and sharp-tailed grouse, and even developed a radio collar for grouse. "It was great work," he says, but in 1980, he was offered a position studying polar bears in Alaska. The rest, as the saying goes, is history.

🐾

In the 1950s and 1960s, the main conservation concern for polar bears was whether they were being overharvested. In Alaska, trophy hunters were using small aircraft to search for polar bears. Once one was spotted, they could land on the ice and shoot the animal. Similarly, trophy hunting from large vessels was becoming popular in Norwegian waters. At the same time, native people continued their traditions of subsistence hunting for meat and fur, and non-native people increasingly were trapping polar bears on Svalbard, north of Norway. "Monitoring was difficult because the hunt occurred far offshore and tallying the harvest didn't effectively account for the increasing number of hours hunters were flying or the ever-expanding geographic areas they were searching," says Amstrup. By the late 1960s it was clear that in Alaska and Norway, and perhaps elsewhere, the number of bears being killed was not sustainable. In 1976, the five polar nations—the United States, the Soviet Union, Denmark,

Norway, and Canada—together signed the International Agreement for the Conservation of Polar Bears, an agreement that, as of 2016, is still the only international treaty focused on a single species. The treaty stopped trophy hunting of polar bears over most of their range. It also meant finding out more about the polar bears and how to assure their long-term survival. The timing, therefore, was good when, in 1980, Amstrup went to Alaska to take over the fledgling polar bear study.

Amstrup had been to Alaska the previous year to work with caribou and had never seen a polar bear; but when asked if he wanted the position, he didn't hesitate to say yes. "I couldn't imagine a riper plum in the wildlife profession than going up to Alaska to study these giant, white bears that roam around in an environment that looks like the surface of the moon," he notes. At this time, little was known about Alaskan polar bears. In the 1970s, much of the research had been on how to actually *do* the research—how to work in the extreme climate with a short field season and great distances to get to the animal. With so little known about these bears, Amstrup essentially began with a blank slate.

❀

Upon arriving in Alaska, Amstrup set up two major objectives: estimating population size and learning where female polar bears built the winter dens in which they have their cubs. His early estimate of polar bear numbers along Alaska's North Slope was about 1,800 bears, but that number alone didn't indicate whether the population was growing or declining. "The trophy hunters pursued the big, older bears. And by the time trophy hunting stopped, few of the largest old bears remained," explains Amstrup. The age structure was heavily slanted toward young bears. By the mid-1980s, however, Amstrup started seeing more of the older animals, including increased numbers of large males. "More older animals was a sign the population was recovering."

Amstrup applied the expertise he had developed in radio-tracking black bears to become the first researcher to successfully use radio telemetry to follow the movements of polar bears, a method that today is being used around the world. This technique was critical because in order to estimate a population's size, you first have to identify its spatial extent. Amstrup and his colleagues pioneered new methods to analyze movements and distributions of highly mobile animals.

About the bears themselves, Amstrup says, "A lot of people think polar bears are aggressive killing machines. My limited experience with grizzly bears suggests polar bears are kind of laid back, and by comparison they have an easier demeanor." An easier demeanor doesn't mean a large carnivore that eats prey the size of a human isn't dangerous and that researchers don't have to be careful. However, Amstrup explains, there are a couple of things that make them less dangerous than grizzly bears. "One thing is that they live in wide open habitats, so you're less likely to surprise a polar bear than a grizzly," he explains. "Surprise leads to the most frequent negative encounter with a grizzly—when you're closer than their flight response, which engages their fight response." Although he calls polar bears more laid back than grizzlies, like any species, they are made up of individuals. Amstrup describes some polar bear cubs he has handled as "chainsaws with fur," while others, he says, are curious and some even have snuggled up to him without being sedated.

Of course there are many challenges in working in the Arctic, and Amstrup says one of the biggest challenges facing polar bear researchers is that when you go off to find polar bears you're always heading away from land and away from your comfort zone. A typical research day would start off in a coastal community on the North Slope, where Amstrup and his team would load equipment into the helicopter, then head offshore to start looking for the bears. "We'd fly out until we found the mixture of solid and broken ice that's their preferred habitat and start searching," he explains. "We'd follow footprints with the helicopter until we found the bear. After finding it, we'd shoot it with a dart or projectile syringe loaded with an immobilizing agent. When the bear was safely asleep, we'd land and begin our work. This included weighing, measuring, ear-tagging, and sometimes fitting animals with radio-transmitting collars. Hopefully we'd repeat that sequence of events several times a day, catching as many bears as we could so we could increase our sample size." Not every day was a success, though. Sometimes they'd fly all day long and never see a bear. Other times they'd see bear after bear. "I can't think of many things that are more exciting than polar bear research," says Amstup, and adds, "but sometimes it was long periods of boredom punctuated by giant adrenaline rushes."

Sometimes there was too much excitement, like in 1982 when Amstrup and his team had jet engine failure for the first time. "These days we have satellite phones and GPS locators," Amstrup says, "but in the early years, there wasn't a good way to communicate with land." Down on the ice with a disabled helicopter, Amstrup and his colleagues figured out they could send a Mayday signal on a radio frequency monitored by passenger jets flying over the North Pole to Europe. "We saw a contrail overhead and started broadcasting. Fortunately, we reached an English-speaking pilot who relayed a message to Anchorage and eventually another helicopter came to the rescue." Not only did they have to hitch a ride back to the coast, but they had to arrange for a second, larger helicopter to come out and pick up their downed one. "It was a little bit exciting, but once we made radio contact, we felt better," he says. "There was a lot of snow, and we built snow caves where we thought we'd spend the night. We were a little disappointed that they picked us up before dark and couldn't test just how good our makeshift shelters were, but I'm guessing, based on subsequent nights I've spent on the ice due to bad weather, that we slept better back on shore than we would have out there!"

Despite the occasional chaos of the logistics, Amstrup continued his research and the pursuit of his second main objective—learning about polar bear denning locations and habitat. In doing so, he provided great insights. "In those early days, the prevailing hypothesis was that Alaska only had a transient population of polar bears. It was thought they were being born in Canada or Russia," he says. However, between 1981 and 1992, Amstrup followed radio-collared polar bears to discover that, in contrast to popular belief, polar bears do den in Alaska. Not only did he find dens, but he discovered that more than half of dens used by Alaskan polar bears weren't on land, but on the drifting pack ice. This discovery proved to be important because as years passed and it became clear sea ice was deteriorating due to global warming, Amstrup was able to show that the proportion of dens offshore was declining.

Amstrup also found that many of the bears that did den on land selected places on the Arctic National Wildlife Refuge, where there was (and still is) talk of oil and gas development. That possibility prompted Amstrup and colleagues to observe the responses of bears in dens to various anthropogenic disturbances. For the most part, Amstrup found that polar bears are fairly resilient to disturbances outside their dens. "Everyone thought any industrial development outside their den would hurt them," he says. "We didn't see that. Once in dens, they seemed to be pretty resilient to activities outside their den." Having said that, he notes, "We didn't have data to quantify just how much or how close an activity had to be to cause a problem." He therefore emphasizes that protection of denning habitats is still of utmost importance.

In 1995, Amstrup earned his PhD from the University of Alaska in Fairbanks. He continued his research on polar bears and, in 1996, there was a departmental reorganization and his research position was moved from the USFW to the United States Geological Survey (USGS). At this time, researchers and conservationists were still focused on the polar bear harvest and, to a lesser extent, the oil and gas development in their habitat. But by the late 1990s, it was ever more clear to Amstrup that the real threat to polar bears was climate change.

For years Amstrup and his team depended on both spring and autumn field seasons. The spring season was typically March, April, and early May. At this time of year, the ice is solid and there is abundant daylight. By May, warmer temperatures bring fog and other conditions unsuitable for flying over the ice. But still, he says, "In those early years we had a good two-plus months of workable conditions in spring." The autumn season was typically October and early November. Historically, sea ice froze solid by early October. Because the sun sets for the winter around Thanksgiving time and doesn't reappear until late January, an October freeze-up meant they could work for at least a month before day-length was so short they didn't have time each day to get out and back safely and still capture, radio-collar, ear-tag, weigh, and measure some polar bears. Then, in the late 1990s, things started to change. Amstrup remarks:

> Although each year was different in many respects, we noticed by the late '90s that it was ever more difficult to get any work done in the fall. Whereas we used to have solid sea ice by about October 10, in the late 1990s sea ice was not solid until early to mid-November. By the time the ice was frozen enough for us to work safely, day lengths were too short to be productive. Finally, in 2000 we had to give up the fall season as simply not being cost effective. We have not done that kind of autumn work since then, and in more recent years the warming of the Arctic has shortened even the spring field season.

In each subsequent field season, Amstrup continued to observe how the sea ice was changing. As he observed the changes, global warming and its effect on polar bears became his overarching concern. Amstrup's primary questions were no longer about how many polar bears there were or where they lived or how they lived, but whether or not they would *keep* living—would polar bears be able to survive the impact of climate change, and if so, for how long?

"Contrary to what some people might suggest, our biggest concern is not how polar bears are faring today," Amstrup explains. "It's the future we need to be concerned about." As of 2016, Amstrup and other researchers estimate the worldwide population is between twenty thousand and twenty-five thousand polar bears. Therefore, although some sub-populations are already in trouble, the global population is still relatively large. Amstrup's research shows, however, that if humans continue on our present path of greenhouse gas emissions, two-thirds of the world's polar bears could be gone by 2050. "There is a linear relationship between global mean temperature and sea-ice extent," he explains. "That means that regardless of how polar bears are doing now, if we don't stop the rise in global temperatures, their habitat ultimately will be gone." As for the population in northern Alaska, there is already bad news. "We had a paper come out in 2015 that showed the southern Beaufort Sea population, which I spent the last thirty years studying, had declined approximately 40 percent in the first decade of the 2000s. Clearly that is a sign of a population already in trouble."

The good news is that their path toward extinction can be stopped. In 2010, Amstrup and a team of researchers published a study in the journal *Nature* titled "Greenhouse Gas Mitigation Can Reduce Sea-Ice Loss and Increase Polar Bear Persistence." This paper showed that substantial sea ice could be maintained if we halt the rise in greenhouse gas concentrations. Furthermore, mitigating greenhouse gas rise would allow polar bears to persist throughout the century and, with sufficient mitigation, long after that. "Early modeling that was included in our 2010 paper suggests it might be twenty-five years before sea ice would stabilize after you stopped the rise in emissions," Amstrup says. "The important point is that if we do act soon, the stabilizing of the temperature and the stabilizing of the sea ice will occur in time to save polar bears."

In other words, it's not too late—but only if we act now to cut our greenhouse gas emissions.

Of course polar bears aren't the only Arctic species being affected by global warming. The impacts, however, are most obvious for the ice bear, as they are known in Denmark and Norway, and as such, *Ursus maritimus* has become the poster child for climate change. Amstrup explains:

Polar bears can only predictably catch seals from the surface of the sea ice, so in addition to their mystique, the main reason they have become the face of climate change is because they depend on a habitat that literally melts as temperatures rise. Seals can swim in open water during summers with no ice. When polar bears don't have a surface from which to catch those seals, they are food deprived. Longer summer periods without ice, therefore, mean longer periods without food. Clearly there is a limit to that situation.

Although Amstrup is cautiously optimistic that humanity will "get our act together" and reduce emissions, he is frustrated by the lack of political leadership on the issue. "The United States needs to take the lead," he says. "You often see in the press that China has surpassed the US as the biggest greenhouse gas emitter, but if you look at the historic amount of CO_2 that's in the atmosphere, the US has been the principal contributor. We are still considered a world leader in many areas of social concern to all people, and it's really critical for us to step up on global warming." As shown at the Paris Climate Talks in 2016, the world is ready to take action, but it awaits American leadership.

As for his own role in advocating a curb in greenhouse gas emissions, Amstrup has changed career focus. He worked as a "dyed in the wool" researcher for thirty-eight years, including three decades studying polar bears in Alaska. He has served as chairman of the IUCN (International Union for Conservation of Nature) Polar Bear Specialist Group, authored or coauthored over 150 peer-reviewed articles, and led the USGS research team that was instrumental in getting polar bears listed as a threatened species. "My whole career was centered on research that would provide us a better understanding of our natural world and how we are interacting with it," he says. "But I left research in 2010 because, even though there are still lots of interesting questions to ask about polar bears, we already know the answer to the most important question: What do we need to do to save them? To assure a future for polar bears, we need to stop the rise in the atmospheric greenhouse gas concentrations. Anything else won't work."

After leaving the USGS, Amstrup became the chief scientist at Polar Bear International. There, his mission is to apply his scientific knowledge to the challenge of conserving polar bears and their sea-ice habitat. In 2012, his success in bridging the gap between research and conservation won Amstrup both the Indianapolis Prize (an internationally recognized animal conservation award to celebrate the men and women who have made extraordinary contributions to sustainability of wildlife) and a Bambi Award for conservation (the biggest annual media event in Germany that recognizes excellence in international media and television, but which each year also has an award jury that selects a few people who have made significant humanitarian contributions, major physical achievements, or important strides in conservation). He has been interviewed for countless radio and TV shows including *The Today Show*, *NBC Nightly News*, and *CBS Sunday Morning*, and he has participated in numerous environmental film projects.

Amstup's current work might not be as exciting as studying polar bears in the Arctic, but he describes what he's doing as an opportunity. "The world needs to get the message that this is not just about polar bears. And that if we act in time to save polar bears, it will benefit the rest of life on earth, including ourselves."

In order to promote conservation in his personal life, Amstrup and his wife, Virginia, built an energy-efficient home in northeastern Washington state. "It's a wonderful home with a great view of the local landscape, but it's also built for energy savings and a reduced greenhouse gas footprint," he says. "Between our efficient insulation and the solar panels on our roof, we're nearly energy neutral. We have an all-electric home, but during the first year we lived here, the total electric bill was just 130 dollars!" Although everyone might not be in a position to build a new energy-efficient home, Amstrup believes everyone is in the position to make choices that can help reduce emissions. "If in every choice we make we think about overall impact of the activity rather than just what's most convenient we're likely to make the best choice for the earth," he says.

In his long career, Amstrup has seen that conservation needs a new focus. "Climate change, or global warming, turns our normal models of conservation on their heads," he says. "Historically, if we saw a piece of habitat that was endangered, we could build a fence around it or we could set it up as a preserve, or if there's poaching on a particular species, we could hire more game wardens. But we can't build a fence to protect the sea ice from rising temperatures. So we need to think of this not as a conservation effort that people like me or game wardens or anybody else can deal with on the ground. Polar bear conservation can't be done in the Arctic. It's done down here where you and I live. And it can only be accomplished by changing the way we use energy."

Although Amstrup can't think of many things that are more exciting than polar bear research, these days he can think of things that are more critical to their survival: taking action. But the challenge is daunting, and Amstrup emphasizes that we need help from our policy leaders. Although we all can and should make our own commitments to minimize our personal greenhouse gas footprints, personal commitments alone are no longer likely to get us on the path we need to take to save polar bears. He explains:

> The solution to this quandary and the key to turning the preservation of polar bears from the possible into the probable is a price on carbon emissions. Rather than telling us how fast to drive, or what kind of car, or how high or low we should set our thermostats, if governments did *just one thing*—establish a fair price for carbon emissions—the free markets of the world could sort out the rest. A price on carbon would eliminate current subsidies on fossil fuels and level the playing field for all energy sources. It would make renewable energy more competitive, cover the costs of new technologies, and create a multitude of jobs. And it will assure a future world similar to that in which polar bears and humans have flourished.

There is no future for polar bears without greenhouse gas mitigation. Humans caused the problem, and fortunately, humans still have time to fix it. Amstrup is optimistic we will do so.

For more information on Steven Amstrup, please visit www.polarbearsinternational.org.

CHAPTER 9

• • •

Meg Lowman, PhD:
A Real-Life Lorax

"Trees and mothers have a great deal in common. Trees are the heart of productivity of many ecosystems, just as mothers function as the biological center of birth and life. Like motherhood, trees provide energy and nutrients for the entire community. If only as a mother I could achieve as much as a tree."

—Meg Lowman

Credit: Carlton Ward

Meg Lowman.

SHOULD SHE LEAVE HER CHILDREN at the bottom of the tree with the venomous brown and black snakes, or take them up? This was a question that Meg Lowman, the world's leading expert in treetop ecology and a mother of two, encountered while her boys were young and she was conducting field research in Australia. Taking them up with her meant scaling a tree of up to two hundred feet. When her boys were four and five years old, she got them their own harnesses. Decision made. They'd come with her.

"All of my academic advisors and professors were men, and although they were brilliant," says Lowman, "they definitely did not advise me on issues such as juggling children and field expeditions." How to conduct pioneering research in remote places across the globe while raising children was something she'd have to figure out for herself; she'd be breaking new ground in the process—both as a researcher and as a woman in science.

Throughout her own childhood in rural upstate New York, Lowman was a self-proclaimed nature nerd. She spent hours building tree forts with her friends, rescuing baby birds fallen from their nests, and pressing wildflowers between the pages of the phone book. She loved science, but with no female science teachers or role models, she didn't seriously consider that girls could become scientists.

At age twelve, Lowman wrote to Duryea Morton, the president of the National Audubon Society in New York City, and declared her love of nature. He wrote back and told her about the Burgundy Center for Wildlife Studies in West Virginia, one of the few summer camps in the country dedicated entirely to nature. Lowman's parents enrolled her in the camp, where, among other things, she got to band birds; collect, identify, cook, and consume mushrooms; key trees and insects; and camp under the stars for the first time. Two weeks later, Lowman emerged a new person. She had found her people. The camp, and perhaps her second-place win in the New York State Science Fair ("approximately 499 boys with volcano experiments and me"), encouraged her to think of a career in science.

In the early 1970s when Lowman began college, however, she found being a woman in a scientific field wasn't easy. As a junior at Williams College, juggling a biology and geology major ("I loved rocks as much as plants"), the chair of the geology department made it clear to her that women were not welcome into the senior major tutorial. "In those days we would never consider protesting, so I retreated and majored in biology." Lowman jokes that she was "simply glad to find a ladies' room in the science department," but her obstacles as a woman in science weren't a laughing matter. Later, when she entered a PhD program in the school of forestry at

Duke, she was one of only two women in the department. When she went on to finish her degree at Sydney University in Australia, she encountered the same situation: A male-dominated department, so male-dominated, in fact, the department chair called her in and asked why she was working so hard when she was just going to get married and have children.

With her characteristic determination and persistence, Lowman did not let the sexism she encountered stop her. If anything, these obstacles fueled her to work harder to become not just a pioneer in the field of canopy ecology, but an educator and an advocate of girls and minorities in science. "I feel a true sense of passion to serve as a role model and inspiration for all women in the world. I try to be a good role model for the young women that I encounter, so maybe they can gain advice and avoid some of the hurdles that I encountered."

Lowman speaks passionately about the underrepresentation of girls in science. "Although approximately 51 percent of the planet is female," she says, "less than 10 percent of women occupy leadership roles in all aspects of science and, on average, women scientists, doing the same jobs as men, make two-thirds of a man's salary." In developing countries, such as India or Cameroon, where cultural norms can be obstacles for women to become scientists, the numbers are even starker, with almost no women getting trained to become scientists. One way Lowman has addressed this issue was to write a book called *Life in the Treetops,* which offers stories about the hurdles she encountered, as well as "heartfelt advice of how to get a foot—even merely a toe—in the door of my profession of science." She also mentors women wherever she goes, from the United States to India, from the Amazon to Ethiopia. If a culture requires these women to normally wear saris or skirts, Lowman finds them blue jeans and gets them scaling trees.

Given her commitment to empowering girls and women, it is no surprise that two historical figures Lowman venerates are Rachel Carson and Harriet Tubman. "I admire Carson for single-handedly taking on big industry with her *Silent Spring* message. And I love Harriet Tubman, who was an incredible naturalist and able to navigate in the forests in the dark by feeling the moss on the tree trunks, thus guiding slaves northward during the 1800s."

On top of the challenges she has faced in being a female scientist, her chosen field *within* science has also had major obstacles. Just getting to her research site is a dilemma. In the 1950s, scuba gear was invented.

In the 1960s, a man went to the moon. During all this time, there were no tools for canopy research. Yet, when Lowman realized that over half the forest was beyond reach and sight, she knew she had to figure out how to get into the treetops. "No scientist had ever done this before to my knowledge, so I had to invent my own methods moving forward." It wasn't until March 1979 that Lowman developed the gear for ascending trees. For merely three hundred dollars, she fashioned seatbelt webbing into a harness, forged a slingshot with a piece of metal in the shop at Sydney University, and bought a caving rope. With the tools in hand and no idea how well they'd work, the time had come to climb.

The first step to climbing a tree is what's called rigging—getting the rope over a branch sturdy enough to support human weight. Since that first tentative rig, Lowman has become quite an expert—a skill few people get to put on their resume. Ropes are not her only tools for getting into the canopy, though. Lowman has designed treetop walkways (including the world's first canopy walkway in Queensland, Australia) and has used hot air balloons, cherry pickers, and construction cranes to get into tree canopies—"the action hot spot of the tree"—where one-half of the biodiversity of terrestrial life can be found.

Despite such amazing biodiversity, most of what lives in the canopy is unknown to science. According to estimates, only about 10 percent of what lives in the forest canopy has been discovered, less if you include the more complex forests such as the Amazon. The canopy is so little explored and home to so much life that some biologists have designated it as the "eighth continent." Like any pioneer charting new territory, Lowman and her students are learning about previously undiscovered biological diversity. In the summer of 2013 alone, she and her team discovered eight new species. Another summer she found a caterpillar that was eating 50 percent of the beech trees in Australia. Because the caterpillar lived in the canopy, nobody had ever seen it before. Lowman reared the caterpillar and it underwent metamorphosis in her tiny Sydney living room. "For months, I had jars of beech branches and caterpillars dominating my life and living space. At the end of the field season, I realized I had discovered not just a new species, but also a new genus." Because a genus is a whole group of species collectively, as opposed to a single species, the discovery of one is quite unusual.

It is not just the chance to discover new species in the frontier of biodiversity that interests Lowman. Her passion first and foremost is conservation. Her philosophy of "Save forests first, otherwise you're discovering new species in extinct habitats," drives her work. "The sad thing about our history of clearing forests in America is that we don't really know what used to live in our own forest canopies, or what might be extinct or missing from the secondary forests. We will never know these answers." With that in mind she adds, "It's not good enough to collect data. I want to make people understand how important it is to conserve the forest."

One country where she is working hard to do just that is northern Ethiopia.

With just 5 percent of its original forest left, most of what remains in this part of Africa is Afromontane forests, surrounding Orthodox Tewahedo churches. There are approximately three thousand islands of these remnant Afromontane forests, ranging in size from three to three hundred acres, and some are more than 1,500 years old. These forests are virgin territory for scientists. Nobody has ever surveyed the canopies. But Lowman doesn't just want to study them. She wants to save them. To do so, she has forged an alliance with the spiritual leaders of the churches, the Coptic priests, who believe they are not just stewards of humans, but stewards of all God's creatures. Forging this alliance was an accomplishment in and of itself because the priests were distrustful of white people who had historically tried to convert them or exploit their resources. In this case, Lowman and the priests share a common goal. "What we call biodiversity, they call God's creatures," says Lowman. The label is irrelevant. The mission is the same. "We're both trying to conserve it."

In order to protect these remnant patches of forests from threats that include firewood harvesting, cattle grazing, and agricultural cultivation from a growing population composed largely of subsistence farmers, Lowman has inspired the priests and the people to haul rocks from agricultural fields, making the fields easier to farm, and use the rocks to build beautiful walls around the forests. In this unique partnership of science and religion, Lowman surmises that being a woman has helped her mission. "The priests trust me as a lone woman sharing their values. Now all the priests want walls around their churches."

In addition to the rock walls, the research, the environmental education, and the mentoring of Ethiopian children in schools adjacent to the church forests, she and Worku Legesse Mulat, an Ethiopian ecologist now based in Dallas, Texas, as a research associate with Lowman's TREE Foundation, wrote a children's book, *Beza, Who Saved the Forests of Ethiopia One Church at a Time*. Lowman hopes the sales of the book in the United States will fund the distribution of it in the native Ethiopian language, Amharic, and inspire more local conservation—and more girls in science.

Lowman's other international projects include a canopy research program for Bhutan in the Royal Manas National Park, a biologically diverse gem that is home to Bengal tigers, one-horned rhinos, Asian elephants, common and clouded leopards, golden langurs, and myriad other species. "They are planning a wonderful canopy walkway and field station," says Lowman. "I am excited to be part of a forest sustainability program in a country that not only has 70 percent of their forest intact, but also states clearly in their constitution that the environment needs to be protected."

Lowman's field work in Ethiopia, Bhutan, and the Amazon is all part of her role as director of global initiatives and chair of botany at the California Academy of Sciences—she was previously the first woman to serve as Chief of Science and Sustainability in the Academy's 163-year history. Part of her job at the Academy is to work as a sustainability scientist; another part is to share the mission and the knowledge of their accomplishments with audiences as diverse as schoolchildren and business leaders. Lowman's other achievements include being the founder of the TREE Foundation, winning numerous awards, authoring over 125 peer-reviewed scientific papers, publishing the successful memoir *Life in the Treetops*, and being the mother of two sons, both of whom pursued science in college.

Of everything she has accomplished, though, Lowman's favorite part is still the trees:

> Trees provide life for everything. They are the building blocks of life on earth. In short, we could not live if trees were not part of our environment. Healthy forests mean healthy humans. Trees are the most successful machines that transform sunlight into energy and provide food for all the food chains of life on earth. In addition, they conserve water, reduce soil erosion, provide shade, create homes for up to half of the species of our planet, give us medicines and food and building

materials, provide spiritual sanctuary, and store carbon. And they do all of this literally while we sleep. Unlike babies or pets, we do not need to water and feed them or even get a babysitter when we leave them home alone.

Working in trees presents physical risks, but the heights don't scare her, nor does the equipment. Scaling such heights has become second nature, and the gear is top-notch and well maintained. What is harder for Lowman, a woman who lives to get things done, is "the insidious nature of both conservation and issues surrounding women in science at a global scale. It is tough to stay focused completely on the trees and not on the surrounding politics." Although many people have endured a difficult boss or had to re-boot a big project, in conservation every minute matters and lost time means lost habitat, making any distractions especially frustrating.

It is frustrating, but not enough to slow her down. Like her days in college forging a path as a woman in science, Lowman does not let the hindrances get in her way. She is always looking for a way to solve problems; so much so that some of her friends say "Solution" is Lowman's middle name. Others wonder how she stays so positive when the facts about extinction, deforestation, and climate change are so disheartening.

A philanthropist once asked me what type of antidepressants I took in order to work on such a depressing topic as tropical rain forests and their loss. It is true that this topic is extremely grim and full of gloom and doom, but my children—and young people in general—keep me focused. I do my work for them. We need to leave the world in the best possible condition for the next generation. I am truly focused on solutions. After living in the Australian Outback, figuring out how to access the canopy, and trying to save forests in places like Ethiopia, I strongly believe that a little creative thinking can and will lead to solutions. So I thrive on challenges in the best possible way.

Her only complaint is that she'd like more hours in a day so she could mentor and inspire more women in developing countries, plant more trees, and conserve more forests.

Nevertheless, Lowman makes the most of the time she does have, packing in full days and keeping a frenzied pace with frequent trips that require not just tree-rigging equipment, but things such as malaria medication, mosquito netting, clothes to deter leeches and—in the early days—diapers. In the introduction to *Life in the Treetops* Lowman notes that "My children have been extraordinary in their patience and flexibility, managing to find security despite their mother's frenzied pace." She simultaneously remarks that her work has required sacrifice.

> I don't do fun vacations like all my friends do, and I am not contemplating retirement, so there is no official date for the sunset years when I relax a little bit more. Also, I was not devoted as much to my kids' world of church or sports as many parents are, but I was a devoted volunteer in their science classes. My mom and dad also made sacrifices since I was never able to find a job close to them, and I would love to see them every weekend as they age.

As usual, she puts a positive spin on the situation, adding, "But we talk on the phone a lot."

In 2016, at age sixty-two and with decades of conservation work behind her, Lowman believes everyone can and should pitch in to save the planet. "The power of one is awesome," she says. "Anyone can and should contribute a minute or a lifetime, depending on what is possible. *National Geographic* did a piece about me called "Climbing One Tree at a Time to Save Forests." The message resonated with a lot of my students, giving them hope that small steps can lead to positive solutions." In Taiwan in 2007, for example, after her memoir was translated into Chinese, a national park staff was inspired to build the country's first canopy walkway for research. And when Lowman went to Taiwan to inaugurate the new walkway, she was thrilled to see many female graduate students—all of whom were studying biology—waving the Chinese version of her book at her and asking for an autograph. On another occasion, Lowman allowed children to help her name a new beetle from the Amazon by putting a competition online. The winning name came from a fifth grader, who years later wrote to Lowman to say she was majoring in biology in college. Of all the students she takes into the trees throughout North America, Ethiopia, and the Amazon, many of them will go on to become scientists and to spread the message about trees and conservation.

Spreading this message is vital to Lowman. She believes it is crucial to teach science communication to scientists, so the significance of forests can be communicated widely and to a diverse audience. She also says that we need to accept "virtual nature" as a reality and as a tool for getting people excited about the natural world. "By combining tools such as iPhone apps and mobile devices for field biology, we can engage millions of young scientists. But," she adds, "we need to have both the technology and the outdoor experiences for youth."

Another way Lowman advises people to save forests is through their consumer habits. She wants people to learn about what they buy and how their purchases ultimately affect forest conservation. "Consumers are a big reason the tropical forest is cut down," she says, citing shade-grown coffee as an example of conservation-minded shopping. One of the many advantages of coffee grown in the shade is that it supports biodiversity of birds and other taxa. Soybeans are another product that contributes to deforestation of the Amazon and which Lowman says should be bought from American growers. Bananas, chocolate, wood, palm oil—the list of products that can hurt or support conservation is long, but if consumers are educated, the power of the purse can make a big difference.

With so many budding ecologists in the next generation, Lowman remains positive about conservation. "The future is filled with bright and optimistic young people. That is truly exciting and we need to inspire and engage them," she says.

Lowman would like to be remembered as an inspiration for helping girls and minorities seek careers in science and as a voice for the trees—a Real-Life Lorax, an arbornaut, the Einstein of the Trees.

For more information on Meg Lowman, please visit www.canopymeg.com.

CHAPTER 10

• • •

Richard O'Barry: From Dolphin Trainer to Dolphin Defender

"The dolphin smile is nature's greatest deception."

—Richard O'Barry

Credit: Dolphin Project Archives

Richard O'Barry.

JUST A STREET AWAY FROM the one that bears his name, Richard O'Barry's one-hundred-year-old bungalow stands out amid a sea of South Miami apartments, both because of its small size and the bright yellow, blue, and green with which it's painted. Developers would love to get their hands on this prime piece of real estate and tear it down to make way for high-priced hotels and condos, but O'Barry won't let them. This former Flipper trainer turned dolphin advocate is too much of a fighter for that. O'Barry was not always an activist, but he has always loved the sea, and it was with the sea that his story began.

🐾

O'Barry was born in Manhattan, but moved to Miami Beach, Florida, in 1939, which is where he was raised. Living so near the water, he grew up fascinated by the ocean. "When I was five, I was walking to school with my brother, and I found a one dollar bill on the road," he recalls. "I took the money to the sporting goods store and bought a pair of goggles. Right after school I went to the beach and swam alone around the legs of a pier that is no longer there. A whole new underwater world opened up to me. From then on I was hooked."

Being hooked meant O'Barry took up diving—advancing from store-bought goggles and paddling around piers, to serious scuba and underwater investigation. In 1955, at age sixteen, he joined the navy. He wanted to become a member of the Underwater Demolition Team, but after he joined, he found out you had to be twenty-one to be on that team. Despite this setback, he spent five years in the navy. During his first Christmas holiday, O'Barry had a two-week leave. He used part of that time to take his mother and two brothers to visit the newly opened Miami Seaquarium. "I pressed against the window of the 600,000-gallon main tank, which in those days was filled with cobia, fifteen-foot long sawfish, sharks, and green turtles. It was so surreal," says O'Barry. "I watched a guy wearing a helmet walk around the bottom of the tank, grabbing dead fish from a wire basket and feeding the dolphins and other marine life swimming around him. It was an 'aha' moment for me. I said to myself, 'That's it. I want to work there.'"

Although it took him five years, O'Barry did eventually get a job at the Seaquarium. On his first day of work, he was assigned to be a diver on a capture boat—the toughest job there. This position meant O'Barry would be one of the crew responsible for capturing dolphins from Biscayne Bay for sale to aquariums across the country. "Every capture is violent," he says, describing the operation. "We'd put out a half-mile net. Dolphins would come to the bow of the boat. The net was so big they wouldn't know they were being circled until it was too late. Then we'd bring them back to the Seaquarium and ship them to Chicago or the World's Fair or New York or whatever." O'Barry knew the captured animals were the financial livelihood of the Seaquarium, and he didn't see anything wrong with what he was doing. At the time, nobody, O'Barry included, understood the complex brains and communication of these air breathing, warm-blooded mammals. Many people were still calling them fish.

In 1961, while still working at the Seaquarium, O'Barry was assigned a job that would set the course of his future's work and passion in motion. He was to capture five dolphins. He was told that these five animals had to be in good shape—no scars or shark bites—look similar, and be around the same age. He did as he was told and brought back five dolphins. This quintet would eventually play the part of Flipper in the tremendously successful movies and internationally syndicated television show of the same name.

O'Barry then became the Flipper dolphins' head trainer. He even served as a stunt double for Luke Halpin, one of the actors in the show. While training the dolphins, O'Barry noticed that some of the animals were aggressive. The producers of the show referred to these aggressive animals as "problem" dolphins. Yet O'Barry had a different view. He didn't believe the dolphins were problematic, per se. He believed they actually were frustrated at being forced to act against their nature, and were thus acting out. When the program ended its TV run in 1967, O'Barry continued working off and on with Kathy, the dolphin that played Flipper a majority of the time. Then, in 1970, he received a life-changing call. "The Seaquarium head phoned me to say Kathy was sick," O'Barry explains and then describes what happened next:

> I had been working on another movie, and had not been with Kathy or at the Seaquarium for quite a while. I found her laying on the surface, her body covered in big black blisters. All I could think was, *What have I done?* I leapt into the tank with her and she came to me and I held her in my arms. She was listless. I felt the life go out of her. Her blowhole was covered in foul white foam. I gently pushed my thumb into her blowhole, careful not to let water get in, and pressed my knee against her ribs to try to get her to breathe. But she was dead. I held her for a long time, I don't remember how long. When I let her go, she sank to the bottom. I knew she had made a decision to die. I raced into the director's office, sobbing

uncontrollably, and blurted, "Why are we doing this?" On the way back to my apartment I was thinking only one thought: something had to be done.

Within a week of Kathy's death, O'Barry took action. He tried to rescue a captive dolphin, Charlie Brown, who was living on Bimini Island, the closest Bahaman island to the United States. O'Barry snuck into Charlie Brown's pen in the middle of the night and cut the wires to open the underwater gate. The attempt did not go well. O'Barry was arrested, and Charlie Brown, having lived his life penned up, was too scared to exchange safety for freedom of the wild.

The media attention from the Charlie Brown fiasco helped to put O'Barry in the spotlight, and he used the attention to begin telling the world that capturing wild dolphins and keeping them in tanks for either research or performance was morally wrong. "The cruelty of marine mammals in steel tanks is worse than animals in zoo cages because cetaceans are echo locators and the sounds they make echo back to them from the steel walls and they go crazy in the mind after a while. Most of them stop talking," says O'Barry. "But at that time no one cared. There was no Greenpeace, PETA, or Earth Island back then."

The world of those depressed and stressed captive dolphins stood in profound contrast to the vibrant and playful wild dolphins O'Barry saw in 1972 while on a dive in the Bahamas with Art McKee, the renowned Florida treasure diver. "The water became alive with fins. At first we thought we were seeing sharks," says O'Barry. "I put on my faceplate and put my head in the water. That's when I realized they were dolphins, hundreds of them." O'Barry had never seen anything like this before. After O'Barry and McKee had been in the sea with the dolphins for thirty minutes, storm clouds started to build. McKee got out of the water, urging O'Barry to do the same, but he couldn't tear himself away. When he finally did get back onto the boat, he knew he had to be around those animals more. "Seeing the dolphins close up like that was such an amazing experience. I dreamed about swimming free with wild dolphins again."

O'Barry followed that dream. As of 2016, he still visits the Bahamas to connect with dolphins whenever he gets the chance. His visits to the crystal clear waters forty miles from land are not contrived. The dolphins are not captive. They are wild, and as such, they control any interaction with humans, taking the lead, coming to the boat due to their natural curiosity. "There's no way to describe the feeling I get there," he says about standing with his scuba tank on the sandy ocean bottom with dolphins "flying" around him. Sometimes he plays underwater music for the dolphins—a Strauss waltz is his preference. "the water becomes like liquid music. When the dolphins show up, it appears that they're completely in sync with the music. They're not dancing, but it looks like they are," he says of the experience. "When they get bored, they swim away."

With his love of dolphins and his knowledge of how they suffer in captivity, O'Barry wanted to do something to help those animals confined to steel tanks across the world in what he calls the "dolphin abusement industry," an entertainment industry that, he says, "teaches people that it's okay to abuse nature." On Earth Day 1970, O'Barry founded The Dolphin Project, the mission of which is to educate the public about captivity, to free captive dolphins when feasible, and to end dolphin exploitation and slaughter. Twice he had to close the organization due to lack of funds, but, determined, he fought on. "I remember standing out there alone in front of the National Aquarium in Baltimore and other places with a sign that said 'Free the Dolphins.' I was like a fool standing out there, but my work was about creating a movement," he says. "And it's here now. Captive dolphins have become a mainstream issue."

But for the dolphins languishing in captivity (most of whom are highly intelligent Atlantic Bottlenose dolphins, weighing from three hundred to six hundred pounds and growing to more than eight feet in length), O'Barry's campaigning wasn't urgent enough. "One of the biggest lies told by the likes of SeaWorld and others is that dolphins in captivity can never be released back into the wild," he says. Starting in 1973, when he was actually able to rehabilitate and release his first dolphin, O'Barry has shown the profit-driven naysayers that they are wrong. Since 1973, he has released over two dozen dolphins in countries as far-ranging as Guatemala in 1991 (where two dolphins were working in a traveling dolphin show), Haiti in 1995 (where six dolphins had been captured in the final days of the Jean-Bertrand Aristide government for "tourist and educational purposes"), and South Korea in 2014 (where two dolphins—there were three, but one escaped on his own—were being held in captivity in an aquarium in Seoul), among other countries. About these rescues he says, "I don't always know what to do, and I don't go with a plan. If I stick around, I figure it out."

Although O'Barry and his son Lincoln (a film director, producer, and animal rights activist, born in 1972), will respond to a dolphin in distress anywhere and anytime, there are more dolphins needing help than the father-son team can tend to. In order to guide other animal activists and marine biologists who want to rehabilitate and release captive dolphins, O'Barry wrote *The Protocol For Releasing Captive Dolphins* in 1995, which anyone can access on the Dolphin Project website. O'Barry argues that dolphins, as free ranging, social, sonic, and highly intelligent marine mammals with both sophisticated physiology and a highly developed emotional sense, are severely stressed by captivity. In the protocol he states: "Stress is the result of not enough space, too many people around, and having to play the fool for too long. Stress is also the result of having to live in an artificial world, a world without tides, without the tastes and sounds of the ocean, and without anything that normally makes life worth living."

Thanks to O'Barry's pioneering work, those wanting to help dolphins now have specific steps that they can follow. The first step is to assess if a dolphin can be returned to the wild. If the dolphin meets the requirements for release, extinguishing behaviors associated with captivity—such as feeding with their head out of water—comprises the second step. O'Barry calls this stage "empowering" the dolphin. The protocol details all essential stages of rehabilitation and release to the final stage of post-release tracking of the animal to monitor how it is doing in the wild. And for those people who want to help dolphins, but are not in the position to work for rehabilitation and release, he says, "The most important thing is to stop buying tickets for dolphin shows. That sounds overly simplistic, but it's the best solution. It works. The dolphin show is based on supply and demand—like any other product."

In addition to his work with captive dolphins, O'Barry is also concerned with wild dolphins, specifically with their slaughter in places such as Taiji, Japan, where he visited for the first time in 2003. Since the 1950s, each year starting on September 1, a small group of Taiji fishermen round up thousands of migrating dolphins into an inlet about the size of a football field called The Cove. The day starts in the morning, when the fishermen encounter the dolphins in international waters. They put a pole in the water and bang on it with a hammer, which terrorizes the sound-oriented animals. The dolphins are then driven into The Cove, which is sealed off by nets so they can't escape. O'Barry calls it a veritable Dante's *Inferno* for the dolphins and a genocide.

Once the dolphins are in The Cove, stage one of the operation takes place: those animals deemed most desirable (no scars or shark bites) are captured and sold to the entertainment industry for as much as $154,000 American dollars per dolphin. The biggest customer of these dolphins is the Japanese dolphin entertainment industry, of which O'Barry says there are fifty-one sites. After Japan, the customers are China, Russia, Dubai, and Turkey. The good news is that no place in the United States or Europe buys dolphins that have been captured this way. "It is slow progress, but it's progress," says O'Barry. "We keep showing up until it stops."

Stage two of this devastating operation is the kill. The dolphins that are not sold for entertainment are slaughtered and sold as meat. About the meat, O'Barry says, "During our many campaigns in Japan we received the impression that dolphin meat is considered trashy." The fishermen, though, say providing meat is not their primary impetus for the hunt. Their reason for slaughtering the dolphins is because it's a "form of pest control." The fishermen have been told by the Japanese fisheries that the dolphins eat too many fish and that is the reason for the decline in fisheries. O'Barry argues against this reasoning, saying that declining fisheries is a much larger global problem, one that is directly related to overfishing and pollution. "It's not about providing meat for the Japanese people, and it's not about maintaining tradition or culture," O'Barry says. "It's about eradicating as many dolphin species as possible in order to make the oceans' fish available to themselves."

Besides documenting and bringing attention to the situation in Taiji, O'Barry has advocated for economic alternatives to the slaughter. These alternatives include support to fishermen during a transition away from killing dolphins, promotion of a tourism industry, which includes whale and dolphin watching, and the implementation of sustainable fishing practices.

In 2009, Louie Psihoyos, photographer, filmmaker, and founder of the Ocean Preservation Society, who later directed *Racing Extinction*, made a documentary about the dolphins of Taiji called *The Cove*. The film follows O'Barry in his quest to document the then covert killing practices, and calls for an end to the slaughter. The film won twenty-five major awards, including an Academy Award for Best Documentary Feature at the Eighty-Second Annual Academy Awards.

After *The Cove* premiered, O'Barry's media attention erupted. He was interviewed by Oprah, Larry King, and Anderson Cooper, among others. "The movie has been the best thing for dolphins," says O'Barry. "I take it everywhere I go, and show it to anyone who will watch, because once you see it you can't pretend this isn't happening in Japan." Thanks to awareness raised by *The Cove,* the number of dolphins being slaughtered in Taiji has dropped from about 2,300 annually to seven hundred in 2016, but O'Barry won't be satisfied until the slaughter is declared illegal and not a single dolphin is captured or killed. In order to see this happen, he continued going to Taiji every year, until he was stopped.

On January 18, 2016, immigration officials at Tokyo's Narita International Airport detained and arrested O'Barry. He then served nineteen days in jail. Officials claimed the reason for his arrest and detention was due to an unannounced side trip he had taken to the town of Futo on a previous trip to Japan in August 2015—a claim O'Barry disputes. Although O'Barry had been arrested twelve times before this event, it was always by his own design. "In the past I was arrested for civil disobedience," he says. "This is the first time I was arrested when it wasn't by my own design."

During his nineteen-day confinement, whenever O'Barry was allowed to make outgoing calls, he'd ask about how many boats were going out on the dolphin kill. Had any dolphins been caught? His friends and family worried about O'Barry's health. He worried about the dolphins. "My heart was in *The Cove,*" he says.

After his detention, he was deported and was issued a ban from returning to Japan. "It marked the last time I would step foot in Japan, at least for the short while—a country I have deeply grown to love over many years I have been visiting there," he said on his blog. He adds, "I have filed a lawsuit against the Japanese government for false arrest and deportation." Although he was seventy-six at the time of his arrest and detention, and it was a physical hardship, he calls it a blessing. "It brought so much media attention to *The Cove* and the problems. Yes, it was uncomfortable, but we hit the jackpot. It brought more media attention than the movie did."

For someone who garners so much media attention, O'Barry says he is fundamentally shy and reclusive, and calls himself the most unlikely guy to do what he does. And although what he has been doing for nearly fifty years has been rewarding, it has also come with sacrifice. "I'm constantly separated from my wife and children because I'm traveling so much. And my work is about conflict. It's about clashing with big business and it's hard not to drag your family into that world," he says, and then adds, "My ex-wife would tell you I'm in a triangle: my wife, me, and the issues. My family and I would agree not to discuss the issues and fifteen minutes into dinner, we would be talking about it."

Besides the Dolphin Project, O'Barry has garnered numerous accolades and achievements. He has written two books, *Behind the Dolphin Smile* (1989) and *To Free A Dolphin* (2000). In 1991 he received the Environmental Achievement Award presented by the Committee for the United Nations Environmental Program (US/UNEP). He is a fellow in *National Geographic's* prestigious Explorers Club, a multidisciplinary society that links together scientists and explorers from all over the world.

Despite such successes, O'Barry believes he would have had more influence had he been a veterinarian or had obtained a PhD. "Because I trained Flipper I had clout," he says. "Without the Flipper experience, I couldn't have gotten so far. I know I could have been more effective in fighting these issues if I was a veterinarian or had a PhD degree behind my name." With this hindsight, he tells those wanting to pursue work in wildlife conservation: "Find out what you're passionate about, learn everything you can about the topic, get a degree related to it, and you will be an expert. That will give you power. Then show up. That's it."

Showing up is a motto that O'Barry lives by. "If there is a dolphin in trouble in the world, I could be on a plane today. It's very spontaneous and that's how it works. I will go to Japan or the Solomon Islands at the drop of a hat. Most times when I show up somewhere I'm not sure what I'm going to do until an hour before I do it. Showing up is the first thing."

In 2016, at age seventy-six, O'Barry is still showing up, and he won't stop until the last captive dolphin is released and their slaughter is stopped.

For more information on Richard O'Barry, please visit www.DolphinProject.com.

CHAPTER 11

• • •

George Schaller, PhD:
Global Wildlife Hero

"As we reach for the stars, we neglect the flowers at our feet."

—George Schaller

George Schaller.

"I LIKE TO WATCH ANIMALS and see what they do," says Dr. George Schaller—an understatement coming from the man who many people consider to be the world's leading conservation biologist. Schaller hasn't just spent the last fifty years "watching" animals; he's been a key player in protecting species and ecosystems across the world. He has worked in the tundra of northern Alaska, the volcanoes of Central

Africa, the rainforests of Brazil, the mountains of the Himalayas, and the steppes of Mongolia. But of all the countries in which he has worked, Schaller has spent the most time in China.

He first went to China in 1980 when he was invited to join a team of Chinese scientists studying the giant panda. After a four-year project in which he found out that poaching, habitat destruction, and capturing of the popular animal for zoos were three threats to its survival, he began field research in a new region of the country: the high Tibetan plateau. Drawn to the "luminous landscape, the wildlife, and the Tibetan culture," Schaller has been going back again and again. "Plenty of biologists are watching things in East Africa because it's a wonderful place," he says, "but for the last thirty-five years, I have been going at least once a year with a mixed team of Chinese and Tibetan researchers to the Tibetan plateau." In particular, it is the desolation and solitude of the Chang Tang, the great northern plain of the Tibetan plateau, which has captured his imagination.

Schaller's comfort in remote, little-known landscapes is rooted in a childhood during which he always felt like an outsider. Born in Berlin in 1933, he grew up in wartime Germany. His father was a German diplomat, his mother an American, and he clearly recalls that the other kids didn't trust him. After the war in 1947, when his mother brought him and his younger brother to St. Louis, Missouri, he was once again distrusted. In his book, *A Naturalist and Other Beasts* (2007), Schaller recalls, "Coming from a country that had inflicted unspeakable horrors on the world, I was not cordially received by everyone." He then describes how feeling like an outsider shaped him: "Being forever itinerant and burdened with the melancholy of an outsider, I became perhaps an internal exile with a detached and reticent character."

Being reticent and detached may have originated in Schaller feeling like an outsider, but they are the very characteristics that later came to help him in long, arduous, and often solitary hours of fieldwork. "You need certain personality traits to be willing to go into silence and loneliness, and you have to be willing to adapt. I find my emotional center and am comfortable," he says of his work in some of the most remote places on earth. "Certainly it suits my inner landscape, reflecting a certain self-contained spirit."

Perhaps because he felt like an outsider, Schaller found connection with animals. "Ever since I can remember I liked roaming forests and meadows," he says. "In high school I collected snakes and lizards for my terrarium, and I kept wild pets such as raccoons and opossum. Not until I went to the University of Alaska in 1955 and got to help in the wildlife department did I become aware that one could make a living observing animals and roaming around."

Schaller didn't just get to help in the wildlife department. In 1956 he got to join the team of renowned biologist and legendary conservationist, Olaus Murie, and his wife Mardy on an expedition in northern Alaska's Sheenjek River Valley along the south slope of the Brooks Range. Throughout the summer, this small group of biologists canoed and hiked through the valley, studying, observing, and cataloging the region's prolific flora and fauna. Armed with evidence of the vast biological diversity and importance of this ecosystem, they returned home and spent four years campaigning to protect the great stretch of wilderness. In 1960, President Eisenhower set aside eight million acres as the Arctic National Wildlife Range, which later expanded to become the twenty-million-acre Arctic National Wildlife Refuge—a region that today is still under constant threat from the oil and gas industry.

On that first of many major expeditions, Murie taught Schaller two important lessons that continue to drive Schaller's work. His first lesson was about conservation. "The basic knowledge of any species I collect has to lead to conservation," he explains. "I feel a very strong moral obligation to help protect what I study." He has abided by this lesson throughout his career, resulting in protection for species that include snow leopards, jaguars, giant pandas, tigers, mountain gorillas, and Tibetan antelope, as well as protection for great landscapes across the planet, including large stretches of the Brazilian Amazon, the Hindu Kush in Pakistan, the Shey-Phoksundo National Park in Nepal, and the Chang Tang Nature Reserve in Tibet.

If conservation was his first lesson, emotion was his second. "When you start out in science, you want to collect data and write papers because scientists publish and that's what gives you status, jobs, and grants," says Schaller. As he inventoried species with Murie, gathering everything from mosquitoes (three species) to moss to mice in order to learn about the area, Schaller learned that it wasn't just about collecting and counting species, it was about connecting with a place. "Murie said you have to look at 'the precious intangible.' That is, the beauty, something that touches the heart. Without emotion you can't understand the animals you are observing. You have to look at them with empathy and intuition to try to get into their world. That's part of why people spend years in the field."

Although Schaller has always had an emotional connection to his work and a belief that conservation comes from the heart, he knows that one also needs facts and numbers, the empirical evidence of science, in order to make others listen and to enact change. "The government might say, for example, wolves are bad. With science you can say hey, wait a minute, everything's interconnected. You lose wolves and there will be an impact on the ecosystem—the herbivores will increase and the plants will decrease. It will have a cascading effect." His many conservation accomplishments have come from a combination of concrete data and out-of-the-box imagination. "Every project has the science," he says, "and then I look for the beauty and dream about what I want to see happen in the future."

The currents atmosphere toward science in the United States, however, is something Schaller finds depressing. "The average American citizen doesn't listen to science," he says. "Consider that 40 percent of Americans don't believe in evolution. This country is atypical. Most countries are more open to science."

🐾

After his undergraduate education and fieldwork with the Muries, Schaller went on to earn a PhD at the University of Wisconsin in 1962. It was his advisor and mentor, ornithologist Dr. John Emlen, who suggested Schaller's next scientific study—an expedition funded by the National Science Foundation to the Virunga volcanoes, in what was then the Belgian Congo, to study mountain gorillas. In 1959, at age twenty-six, Schaller set off with his wife, Kay, to study a species that until then had been thought of as a terrifying brute. "When I went overseas to study the mountain gorilla, most said it can't be done, they're too ferocious," recalls Schaller. "My feeling was that I had met all sorts of animals, from bears to wolves, and they weren't ferocious. You just have to get accepted by them. Animals are individuals. If they had bad experiences with humans, they can kill you. The reason animals are so afraid of us is because we have made them so."

In his career of more than half a century, it is an encounter with a gorilla that he describes as his most memorable interaction with a wild animal. "I usually climbed into a low branch of a tree so I could look down into the thick vegetation to watch them," he says. "One day a female climbed up into the tree and sat on a branch next to me. We were about two feet from each other. She had been seeing me day after day for a few months, so she obviously knew I meant no harm. We were both nervous and we glanced at each other and looked away, then she descended." The experience was proof that the gorillas had accepted him.

The results of his work with mountain gorillas between 1959 and 1960, during which time he made regular observations of their diet, social structure, and habits, were his PhD dissertation and also two books that conveyed the intelligence and gentleness of these animals: *The Mountain Gorilla: Ecology and Behavior* (1964) and *The Year of the Gorilla* (1965). Thanks to Schaller, and later the American zoologist Dian Fossey, the myth of gorilla as brute has been dispelled.

Travels in both the Arctic and Central Africa led Schaller to the realization that he did not want to be an academic or university professor. He did not want to study animals in a controlled environment like a laboratory; he wanted to be in the field. To do so, he says, "I've grabbed at every opportunity. I also married someone who liked to be in the field in places like Pakistan, India, and Tanzania."

After spending time with gorillas and coming to the realization about what he wanted to do with his career, Schaller became a conservation nomad. Largely funded by the Wildlife Conservation Society, in the past four decades he has traveled to India to study tigers; to Tanzania to study lions; to the Himalayas to study wild sheep, goats, and snow leopards; to Brazil to study jaguars; to Mongolia to study wild camels and Mongolian gazelles; to Laos to study the saola (a rainforest-dwelling hoofed mammal); to Pakistan, Afghanistan, and Tajikistan to study the Marco Polo sheep; and of course to the Chang Tang highlands of the Tibetan plateau, the site of his passion for the past three decades.

🐾

Long before Schaller first visited Chang Tang, he dreamt of going there, studying the routes of the first Westerners who had been there. The fact that there were no roads, no foreigners, and virtually no people did nothing to stop his desire. If anything, for a man who seeks remote places and overlooked species, it fueled it. In reflecting on his attraction to remote places, he says:

> Things don't look so good when you look at the fact that over 90 percent of land vertebrates are domestic livestock and people. It seems like wildlife is rather outnumbered. I look at the fact that we will have four billion more people in a few years and the fact that there are few leaders who will speak up on behalf of the environment. I can give endless statistics about all the bad that is happening, but I focus on where I can have an impact. There is still quite a bit left, so I pick areas where I can do some good. Areas where there is still space and where there are young scientists who are passionate.

Chang Tang, covering the northern part of the Tibet Autonomous Region (a large province in southwestern China), and extending into western Qinghai province and the southern rim of the Xinjiang Uyghur Autonomous Region (located in the northwestern edge of China), is one of those areas. The average altitude of the massive, high plateau is 14,500 feet, extending to elevations of over twenty thousand feet in the mountains. As such, the weather and working conditions are severe. In order to study the wildlife inhabiting the region, Schaller lives in a tent in winters reaching as low as negative 30 degrees Fahrenheit, and he braves the summer muds caused by snow melt that makes vehicular travel difficult.

In the approximately forty months Schaller has spent in Chang Tang, he has sought to learn more about the little known wildlife of the region. One of those species is the chiru, or Tibetan antelope, an animal whose migration Schaller calls one of the last great migrations of a hoofed animal in Asia. Before Schaller's studies, little was known about the migration of the chiru, yet, he says, "To know about the movements of an animal is the first step in protecting it."

Before the 1990s, when an expensive shawl called a *shahtoosh*, meaning "king of wool" in Persian, came into fashion, chiru numbered about a million. However, when wealthy buyers in India, the United States, and other countries started paying thousands of dollars to wear a shawl made from the chiru's soft, warm, fine wool, the animal's numbers plummeted. Although some stores claimed that *shahtoosh* wool was shed from Ibex and picked up by local people in the mountains, Schaller and his colleagues discovered that in order to make the shawls, hundreds of thousands of chiru were being massacred. By the mid-1990s there were only about seventy-five thousand chiru left. The animal seemed destined for extinction.

Schaller and his respective Tibetan, Han, and Uygur coworkers alerted the government to the mass slaughter of the chiru, which eventually led to their active protection—although today poaching still remains a problem. Besides gaining security for the animal, Schaller also uncovered an important aspect of their biology. After years of fieldwork, he was able to find the chiru's calving grounds, another critical piece in their conservation. Schaller and his colleagues were also key players in getting the Chang Tang landscape protected as a huge Chinese nature reserve. At 300 thousand square miles, Chang Tang is now the second largest nature reserve in the world.

After fifty years of global conservation work, Schaller has an impressive resume. He has written sixteen books, including three on his work and life in Tibet, as well as hundreds of popular and scientific articles. He is a senior conservationist at the Wildlife Conservation Society and vice president of Panthera, an international conservation organization devoted to the conservation of the world's thirty-seven species of wild cats. He has been awarded many accolades, including the National Geographic Society's Hubbard Medal for lifetime commitment to wildlife conservation, the Tyler Prize for Environmental Achievement, Japan's International Cosmos Prize, the International Society for Conservation Biology's Distinguished Service Award, an Indianapolis Prize, a World Wildlife Fund's Gold Medal for conservation, China's Baogang Environmental Prize, the Wildlife Conservation Society's Beebe Fellowship, a Guggenheim fellowship, and a National Book Award in science for his 1973 book *The Serengeti Lion*.

Despite such remarkable accomplishments, Schaller prefers to be simply called a field biologist, or better yet, a naturalist. "I am more of a nineteenth century naturalist," he says of himself. The key difference is Schaller does not want to collect specimens, as did earlier naturalists like Darwin and Audubon; he wants to protect them. He wants to conserve populations of every species in its ecosystem. Besides his roles as a naturalist, conservationist, and author, another label Schaller gives himself is that of "ecological missionary," preaching the gospel of conservation. Of all his roles, Schaller gets the most pleasure when he is in the mountains, observing and taking detailed notes. "Research among the mountains affords the purest pleasure I know," he says. "One which goes beyond the collecting of facts to one that becomes a quest to appraise our values and look for our place in eternity."

He laments that more and more universities are substituting field courses with time in front of a computer. "In nature," he says, "you are required to look and look and look." Schaller believes that emerging ecologists spend more time at desks analyzing GPS data and DNA samples than in the field. While he gives credit to the important work these people are doing and the advances in conservation that these technologies allow, he maintains that without a solid foundation in natural history, conservation is ultimately losing out. In a 2010 interview for *On Wisconsin Magazine*, he said, "Natural history is the basis of knowledge. Unless you go out and study what's in the field, you can't plan for conservation that well. You can measure how fast the forest is being destroyed, you can measure the biomass of grasslands, but you don't know any details."

Another aspect of conservation science where he sees himself as differing from some other scientists is in regard to focus. While many scientists narrow their focus over time, homing in on a particular species or issue, Schaller has stayed broad. "My personality is that I get restless after a while, and I look for something new," he says. Had he chosen an academic career, he wouldn't have been able to sustain such breadth of study and disappear into the field for such long stretches of time, living and exploring in the remote places close to his heart. And of course he wouldn't have been able to have this lifestyle without his wife Kay, who has shared his passion for remote places and about whom he says, "I was extraordinarily lucky to have met her." It wasn't just Kay who came into the field with Schaller; it was his two sons, Mark and Eric, whose childhoods included living in India, Pakistan, and Tanzania.

Of all the different things Schaller has done and of all the species he has studied, Schaller most wants people to remember something that unites us all, humans and non-humans alike: interconnection. "The basic thing to remember is that we are wholly dependent on species, on the natural community for survival," he says. "When we destroy nature,

Conservationists in the Wild

Dr. Thomas Lovejoy, the father of Biological Diversity. Credit: World Wildlife Foundation.

Dr. Anne Innis Dagg and a beloved giraffe. Credit: Anne Innis Dagg.

Israeli ornithologist, Dr. Yossi Leshem.
Credit: Hagai Aharon.

Dr. Kushal Konwar Sarma in the field.
Credit: Lisa Mills.

Dr. Laurie Marker in Namibia. Credit: Cheetah Conservation Fund.

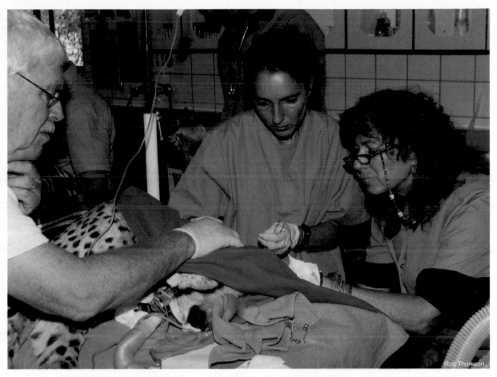

Dr. Laurie Marker operates on a cheetah. Credit: Cheetah Conservation Fund.

Beverly and Dereck Joubert. Credit: Wildlifefilms.co.

Wildlife photographer Paul Hilton. Credit: Paul Hilton Photography.

Dr. Meg Lowman spreads her love of the wild to young children. Credit: Meg Lowman.

Dr. Steven Amstrup with polar bear cub. Credit: Steven Amstrup, Polar Bears International.

Dominque Bikaba. Credit: Dominque Bibaka, Strong Roots Congo.

Richard O'Barry, dolphin defender. Credit: Dolphin Project Archives.

Grace Ge Gabriel speaking on behalf of animal rights. Credit: IFAW.

David Parsons. Credit: Keli Hendrix.

Dr. Megan Parker with Pepin. Credit: Dave Hamman.

Farwiza Farhan in the Leuser Ecosystem. Credit: Paul Hilton Photography.

Dr. Craig Packer. Credit: Craig Packer.

Dr. Dee Boersma with a Galápagos penguin. Credit: Dee Boersma.

Dr. Mike Chase and an African elephant. Credit: Elephants without Borders.

we destroy ourselves. Everything we need, we want, we use, and we buy comes from nature. So we must protect all species and try to mitigate problems."

Despite the interconnection of all life, many people are disconnected from nature, and this worries Schaller. "At least half of the United States is urban now," he says. "You don't meet too many mountain lions or grizzlies in Connecticut (where he lives). People are not used to being in the undisturbed wild. Schools usually don't take children into the woods, but children are very interested in going outside. They should wander around a little. Collect spiders. Watch birds. We must inspire them before they reach their teens when the average kid spends hours on their cellphones instead of poking around in nature. Many communities have a nature center or some research from a university or a cleanup project. Volunteer and get involved." As for his own way of thinking about advocating change and promoting conservation, he says, "I don't deal in hope. I deal in action to accomplish something. I don't sit around hoping."

Getting involved is more than just reestablishing a connection to nature; according to Schaller, it's also a way to meet people who are similarly oriented. For university students, Schaller says, "Go to a department and say 'I'm here to help.' That's what I did, and I found out something important. In Alaska I analyzed the scats of wolves and cleaned their skulls. And I learned that the Fish and Wildlife Service was killing many wolves for no good reason."

After fifty years of fieldwork and conservation, Schaller says, "I don't have any long-term scientific projects right now. I am a so-called 'older statesman' promoting conservation rather than gathering lots of new facts." Keeping with his characteristic humility, even this statement is an understatement. In the fall of 2016, Schaller retraced the 1973 trip he did with author Peter Matthiessen into the Dolpo region of Nepal, which resulted in Matthiessen's famous book and winner of the National Book Award for Nonfiction, *The Snow Leopard* (1978). Although Matthiessen died in 2014, his son, Alex, who was eight years old at the publication of the book, accompanied Schaller, as did photographers Beth Wald and Peter Werth, who run the nonprofit organization Himalayan Currents. Thanks in part to Schaller's efforts, the area he and Matthiessen surveyed was made into a thousand-square-mile national park, but like everywhere in the world, there have been changes. "I wanted to do the trip because I was curious," he says. "There are NGOs providing medical help to communities, building schools and providing solar panels, and I wanted to see what the changes were." At age eighty-three, a trek into the Himalayas might be daunting, but Schaller says, "We did the trip a little easier by flying partway into an airstrip, and I climbed up and down mountains to get in shape beforehand."

Schaller would like to be remembered for the work he did in encouraging young people to continue doing conservation. "This," he says, "will be my lasting legacy." His legacy extends far beyond the human realm, though, and into the myriad species and ecosystems that have gained protection thanks to the vision and the blend of heart and science from a naturalist and writer who has dreamed big and then turned his dreams into action.

For more information on George Schaller; please visit www.panthera.org and www.wcs.org.

CHAPTER 12

• • •

Grace Ge Gabriel: Chinese Champion for Animals

"I want to let people know that animals have feelings, they can suffer pain, and it is our responsibility to make the world a better place for them."

—Grace Ge Gabriel

Grace Ge Gabriel.

Based on stories she'd been told about the vicious nature of the man-eating tiger, Grace Ge Gabriel should have been afraid. It was dusk in February 2004. For hours, she and legendary Indian conservationist Ashok Kumar had been hoping to glimpse a Bengal tiger. Suddenly the forest erupted with noise. Monkeys screamed. Birds chattered. All the animals near them seemed to be looking in one direction. And then they saw it, a large silhouette on the hill, moving slowly toward them. As the silhouette got closer, they realized it was a tiger dragging a sambar deer in her teeth—and she was heading straight for them. "We had to back up the jeep to give her the right of way," recalls Grace. "Ashok thought she must be going to feed her cubs."

As Grace watched the tiger drag its prey past their jeep, she wasn't afraid, and she didn't see the animal as threatening. "I'd been working to stop the tiger trade, and I just felt for her because she was so vulnerable. A tiny drop of poison could kill her, and this was the moment where I felt how important the work of saving wildlife is."

🐾

Perhaps another reason that Grace, the driving force behind the International Fund for Animal Welfare (IFAW) in China, an organization that works to rescue and protect animals in over forty countries around the world, wasn't afraid of the tiger was because of her special connection to the animal. Grace was born in the year of the tiger, and her mother always said that she was one. "I was born at dusk—when tigers hunt—and I am tenacious. If I decide on a goal, I will chase it down relentlessly—like a tiger."

The tiger is a pride of the Asian continent and is deeply embedded in Chinese culture. Images of tigers have existed since antiquity in Chinese literature and art. The animal is so important and revered that it is part of the Chinese Zodiac—every twelve years a tiger year comes along. Yet their habitat is less than 7 percent of its original range, and there are fewer than 3,200 tigers left in the wild, a sharp decline from about 100 thousand a century ago. Scientists believe that China is the origin of all subspecies of tigers. Even so, Gabriel says, "After years of hunting and using their body parts, look at China today, it hardly has any tigers left in the wild." Reversing this decline is one of the many wildlife conservation and welfare projects with which Grace has been involved during her twenty years of work with IFAW. "There are literally a few individual Siberian tigers on the border of Russia and China. Sometimes, they will roam across the border into China and then they face a serious threat from snares, poison, and lack of food. In the spring of 2014, we supported a de-snaring campaign in the Hunchun region of China. In a matter of twenty days, the team found 1,800 snares, many still attached to wild boars or deer carcasses, their target victim."

Snares killing prey species are just one of the many problems tigers face. A larger and more menacing threat is direct poaching for the trade in tiger parts and derivatives. Tiger bones have been used in traditional Chinese medicine (TCM) for centuries. Three thousand years ago, Chinese medicine's pharmacopeia included tiger bone as an ingredient for treating certain illnesses. Although China's State Council banned the use of tiger bone in TCM and took it off the pharmacopeia in 1993, businesses started breeding tigers for the trade of their parts, stoking residual demand. "Unfortunately, China's Wildlife Protection Law is so pro-utilization that it allows farming endangered species for commercial trade," explains Grace. "The law is not based on protecting wildlife because they contribute to ecosystem health, but because wildlife species have 'economic and cultural value.'"

That phrase "economic value" basically tips any conservation law on its head, promoting captive breeding and allowing an even higher number of endangered animals to be used for commercial purposes. So while China's State Council banned tiger bone and rhino horn use in TCM, the law allows corporations to speed-breed tigers to produce tiger bone wine, thus creating a new market for tiger products.

Grace respects the holistic and precautionary approach in TCM, and as such, has worked with TCM practitioners to use plant-based alternatives to replace the 3 percent of TCM ingredients that come from animals. While promoting the use of alternatives by suppliers, she also realizes the importance of changing consumer attitudes. "In order to protect species, we have to change people's behavior at every link on the trade chain," she says. With the growth of the Internet in China, Grace and IFAW have started doing just that. For example, they helped a group of Chinese conservationists set up a website called "Love Tiger," with the purpose of educating the public against the use of tiger parts and to remind Chinese consumers of the importance of the tiger in their culture.

Although Western social media platforms such as Facebook, Twitter, Instagram, or YouTube are not available to users in China due to government censorship, Chinese companies have been developing their own social media products. WeChat, developed by Chinese Internet giant Tencent, is one such product. With over seven hundred million users worldwide, Grace hopes more Chinese will use WeChat to spread the message of animal welfare and ethical consumption. "Social media has made the world smaller. No matter where you are, whichever social media platform you are on, if you have a following, please spread the word," she says. "Educate others—spread the message of kindness and compassion. Influence your friends and family. Social media has given everyone a voice. And our voices matter if we want to mobilize society for wildlife."

Grace's effort to educate and raise awareness about conservation is not just related to the tiger. When she and her colleagues at IFAW conducted a survey in 2007 and found out that 70 percent of Chinese people were unaware that ivory came from dead elephants, Grace had a realization: People were not prejudiced against elephants; they were simply uninformed. In Chinese, elephant ivory is called *xiang ya*, which translates as "elephant teeth." This name has given people the false impression that, like human teeth, elephant ivory falls off naturally, without the elephant dying. That same survey contained a very optimistic prospect: 83 percent of the respondents said they would not buy ivory if they knew it came from dead elephants. Grace and her colleagues took action. They started an advertising campaign called "Mom, I have Teeth," to let consumers know the true cost of ivory. A Chinese executive from a global advertising agency saw the campaign and gave IFAW free space to put the poster all over the country.

"In my line of work, we do see a lot of things that are really discouraging, but I relish the moments when I know I have influenced a change even in just one person," says Grace. With "Mom, I have Teeth," she has witnessed such changes. "I heard from an ivory carver, who promised to use other materials to replace ivory, and a young mother who took a picture of our poster in the subway and posted it to a young mothers' forum. She said she felt so embarrassed that she was wearing an ivory bracelet when she saw the poster and now she tells her friends that every piece of ivory comes from a dead elephant." The poster even touched an educator who put the message into China's College Entrance Exam language test, subsequently reaching nine million college applicants across the country.

In 2013, IFAW conducted an evaluation of the "Mom, I have Teeth" campaign and found that 75 percent of urban Chinese had seen it and the posters reduced the group with the most propensity to buy ivory from 54 to 26 percent.

Grace's work on elephant awareness has gone beyond "Mom, I have Teeth" and has made its way into schools. Each year IFAW chooses one animal theme to educate students about. One year, the theme was elephant protection. After teaching the children about the ivory-elephant connection, they asked students to get a family pledge to reject ivory. "One boy went home and asked his parents to sign the pledge," says Grace. "His father refused to sign, so the boy went on a hunger strike. Chinese children like this boy are little emperors and empresses—single child families who have two sets of grandparents caring for them, and if they miss one meal, it is going to cause great concern and aggravation. So because of the child's hunger strike, the family relented and signed a pledge not to use ivory!" Young people, Grace believes, have the power to influence change and to inspire others, and not just through hunger strikes. "Kids today are better in getting their message out to the world. They have social media. Our key is to inspire and encourage them to do more to get the message out."

Going beyond just raising awareness, Grace believes that policy, advocacy, and society mobilization are equally important approaches in bringing about behavior change. In November 2014, IFAW launched a new campaign called "Give Peace to Elephants, Say NO to Ivory." Over a dozen key opinion leaders (KOL) from throughout Chinese society—artists, music icons, media stars, businessmen and women—lent their voices to the campaign. Speaking from their heart and in one voice, they urge both individuals to reject ivory and the government to ban ivory trade. Through social media, indoor and outdoor posters, and on airwaves and television, they influence their peers, friends, families, and millions of fans.

In September 2015, Grace took a group of Chinese wildlife ambassadors led by CCTV host Yue Zhang, a KOL, to Kenya to see wild elephants and influence the behavior of Chinese communities in Africa, kicking off the "China Africa Wildlife Ambassadors" initiative. "The role of these Chinese wildlife ambassadors is to encourage Chinese citizens in Africa to obey local laws, reject wildlife consumption, and become champions of China's image abroad," Grace explains. "These wildlife ambassadors also influence policy by building a coalition of government and business leaders who understand how wildlife crime undermines China's long-term investment in Africa." Groundbreaking policy shifts happened when, in September 2015, President Barack Obama and

President Xi Jinping jointly pledged to "take significant and timely steps to halt the domestic commercial trade of ivory" in both countries.

These successes have given Grace hope, but change takes time. "Now 75 percent of Chinese know ivory is from a dead elephant, but for people with that knowledge to change their behavior, social norms need to change. Strong and clear policies banning ivory trade combined with vigorous enforcement and meaningful penalties for violators will help attach a stigma to ivory consumption. We will only achieve sustained behavior change when ivory consumption becomes socially unacceptable."

Grace's childhood profoundly influenced her decision to devote her life to animal welfare. During Mao Zedong's regime, anybody who spoke up against Mao's policies could be labeled "counter-revolutionary" and put in prison. Millions of people, mostly intellectuals, were persecuted simply because of their ideas. Grace's father was one such person. Labeled a rightist, he was sent to a labor camp where he almost died. He was then sent north to work in a factory. Her mother's path was just as hard. After the universities were closed during the Cultural Revolution, her mother, a professor, was sent to the countryside in the south to be "re-educated" by the peasants. Grace traveled back and forth between her parents, and, at age eleven, started making the three-night, two-day train journey on her own.

It was in the countryside with her mother where Grace had her first taste of animal cruelty—a defining moment in her young life. Grace's family had always owned dogs, but when the Communists took over the country, dogs were labeled as bourgeois, and the government subsequently banned the keeping of them as pets. Instead, they were slaughtered. Although dogs were not allowed in urban areas, they were not banned in the country. "I had a mutt that someone bought me at the market for two dimes, so we named him Two Dimes," says Grace. "My mom and I took care of him and he became my companion. He would guard the apple orchard where my mother worked, and because he was protective of the orchard, people killed him. I remember the day he came home to me on his last breath, and I watched him die in front of my eyes."

The Cultural Revolution ended in 1976, and in 1977 the college entrance exam was reinstated, meaning anybody, no matter what their family background was, could go to college as long as they passed the exam. In 1980, Grace was one of the mere 3 percent of Chinese students accepted into university. She attended Beijing Broadcasting Institute, now called Communications University of China, graduating in 1984 with a bachelor's degree in arts. In 1986, she moved to the United States to obtain a master's degree in communications at the University of Utah.

After graduation, Grace worked as a news editor for KSL, an NBC affiliate television station in Utah. During this time her boss introduced her to the work of IFAW. Grace started using her vacation time to help IFAW, and other organizations, investigate wildlife markets and film animal welfare projects.

Grace knew she wanted to do something to help promote animal welfare in China, and her chance came in 1996 when she went back to China to document nine Asiatic black bears that had been rescued from bile farms in Panyu, Guangdong province. (Bear bile is an ingredient in TCM. China started to farm bears for their bile in the 1980s. Bear bile extraction is a process that involves inserting tubes into the abdomens of bears and "milking" them, sometimes for decades.) "I watched these bears, that had spent their lives in cages while their bile was extracted from them on a daily basis, be released," she explains. "The bears were hesitating on the concrete path, reluctant to touch the lush green grass and feel the soft warm soil because they were deprived of that basic freedom for years. That scene touched me so much."

After this experience, Grace knew she had to have a career helping animals. "I wanted to let people know that animals have feelings, they can suffer pain, and it's our responsibility to make the world a better place for them," she explains. "Seeing the sufferings of animals due to the ignorance of people, I felt that I could really do something about that. The fact that there was no animal welfare organization in China and the concept of animal welfare was very little understood could be seen as challenges, but I saw them as opportunities. I saw China then as a piece of white paper, on which I could design campaigns and projects to enlighten my countrymen about animal welfare."

In 1997, Grace persuaded Brian Davis, the founder of IFAW, to let her set up an office in China. He agreed, and she returned to live in China full time. Instantly she faced challenges getting people to understand the very concept of animal welfare. "The words 'animal welfare' would quite often evoke the wrong questions. People who see welfare

as a luxury they didn't have, and would ask 'What about my welfare?'"
explains Grace. "So we translated the name IFAW into Chinese as the
International Fund for Love and Care of Animals. This way, we are able
to put the responsibility on people to provide the very basic needs that
animals deserve." But it was not just the word welfare that posed a problem in getting people to treat animals with kindness. "The word *animal*
in Chinese literally means 'moving object,'" says Grace. "Just with that
word itself people do not see animals as living, breathing beings that
have emotional feelings and can feel pain."

In China today, there is a combination of new and old—the newly
rich and the old system of TCM—making the situation for wildlife dire:
the country has the highest demand for wildlife products of anywhere in
the world. For many years Grace has asked herself what went wrong with
Chinese culture. How did Chinese people become so cruel to animals?
She has spent many years pondering and researching these questions.

Until one hundred years ago, China had tigers and many other
species because there was a concept of sustainability, of compassion.
Chinese philosopher ZhuangZi (369–286 AD) founded the idea of
people living in harmony with nature, which may have been the first
concept of sustainability. "However, all that has been lost in recent
history because of war, foreign invasion, civil unrest, and because of so
many political campaigns since the Communists took over," says Grace.
"Chinese no longer have the connection to or the awareness of the natural environment. Political campaigns, one after another, changed it all
by eliminating religion, belief, and breaking people's spirits and family
relationships."

Despite the obstacles of economics and politics, in recent years,
Grace has noticed the word "welfare" pop up in the media. She has also
noticed a change in attitude toward how people use the word "it" when
writing about animals. "You can write 'it' two ways in Chinese," Grace
explains. "One way is as an object and the other way embodies a living
thing. Today when people write about animals I am seeing more of the
second definition."

🐾

Making the decision to commit her life to animal welfare has required
great personal sacrifice for Grace, who now lives in the United States.

"I travel for work all over the world, and I am often away from my family, and so I am not able to take care of my parents (who live with Grace and her husband) or my own cat and that weighs on me. My family and husband are very supportive of my work, and I am very lucky in that way."

With sacrifice has come a long list of successes for a woman still in the middle of her career. In 2001, Grace started the first raptor rescue center in China. In 1999, she spearheaded the campaign to protect the Tibetan antelope and started a project to protect the habitat for China's last Asian elephants. She has been involved in various projects to provide emergency relief to animals in disasters. She has testified before the European Union Commission on protecting wild tigers as well as before the UK Parliament Environment Audit Committee on escalating global wildlife crime. In addition, Grace has published articles on conservation and wildlife in numerous books, journals, and magazines.

Over the years of her work, Grace came to realize that focusing on saving one species at a time isn't a fast enough way to implement the sort of systemic change that she is ultimately after. Her focus has grown from campaigning about a single species to campaigning about "ethical consumption." The increase in consuming power in China creates pressure on wildlife all over the world. Uses for wildlife now include medicines, clothing, foods, private collections, trophy hunting, souvenirs, gifts, and even investments. "There is no stopping consumerism," she says. "We have to tie consumers' behavior to policy and law. People don't want to go out looking for endangered species, especially if they are illegally traded, but if you have a policy that allows the endangered species to be legally traded on the market, then consumers, who have no idea in the first place, take market availability for legality." Changing policy is part of what gives Grace hope and why so much of her attention is also on the policy level. "Yes, social change takes a long time, but government action can change things overnight."

Grace literally saw change happen overnight on December 4, 2011, when she and others at IFAW found out about an endangered species auction at a Beijing hotel, walking distance from their office. Grace and her colleagues went to the auction preview and confirmed the wildlife products that were about to go under the gavel. Acting on IFAW's tip-off, the government shut down that auction and issued a notice banning the auction of tiger bone, rhino horn, and elephant ivory. "In the year 2012, the overall mainland China auction volume dropped by 40 percent from the previous year," she says. And not just auction markets—the online trade ban of endangered species by China's e-commerce sites resulted in a sustained reduction of wildlife parts and products traded on these markets, according to IFAW's bimonthly monitoring.

Fighting on so many fronts takes more than just dedication. "The qualities that have helped me are my tenacity and the ability to see the good in people and believe that people are able to change and that I can affect that change. And then having the confidence of doing it," says Grace. "And staying hopeful. I see change in every way. I see government measures to reduce consumption of shark fins, the young kid on a hunger strike, the word for animal changing from object to a living being."

Grace knows that it takes everyone to make lasting change. She can spearhead new initiatives, but everyone needs to be involved—and everyone can be. "Animals are all around us," she says. "Our behavior affects them. Don't just point a finger at other countries and blame the behavior of others. The best way to influence change is to set a good example. The US needs to be a mentor to follow and to set good examples. If you have five minutes, spread the word. Tell a friend or a family member. If you have more time, dig into an issue. Find your conviction. Speak up. We all need to look into our own lives and see what we can do to change what humans are doing to animals."

From tigers to elephants, Grace is spreading the word of animal welfare around China, one person at a time, and it is one person at a time where the world can make a difference.

For more information on Grace Ge Gabriel, please visit http://www.ifaw.org/united-states/about-us/conservation/grace-ge-gabriel.

CHAPTER 13

• • •

David Parsons: Carnivore Conservation Biologist

"There are some who can live without wild things and some who cannot."

—*Aldo Leopold*

Credit: Keli Hendrix.

David Parsons.

IN THE MID-1800S MEXICAN WOLVES freely roamed the mountains and mesas, the arroyos and hills of the Southwestern United States. Following their complete eradication in the mid-1900s, and a subsequent federal program to restore them fifty years later, only ninety-seven of these animals existed in the wild at the beginning of 2016.

Despite being listed on the endangered species list since 1976, *el lobo,* as the Mexican wolf is known in southwestern lore, continues to be threatened by illegal killings, legal removals from the wild due to conflicts with livestock, a lack of genetic diversity, and most of all by politics. A snare of politics and paperwork almost led to their extinction; the perseverance of one man kept that from happening: Dave Parsons.

❧

Born in 1947, Parsons was raised in rural central Iowa on a 240-acre family farm where they grew corn, soybeans, oats, and clover; raised hogs and chickens; and kept a small herd of dairy cattle. "Family farms were the predominant farming practice of the times," says Parsons. "But it wasn't long before that paradigm phased out. Corporations moved in, land prices went up, and it became difficult to make it on a small-scale family farm."

Urged by his father to pursue higher education, Parsons attended Iowa State, but when he got there, he didn't know what he wanted to study—yet he knew he loved the outdoors. When Parsons heard about the fisheries and wildlife biology major, he thought that sounded like a good profession. "It turned out to be the perfect fit for me," he says. When he graduated in 1969, the Vietnam War was in full swing. Parsons drew a low number in the draft lottery but got lucky with his assignment. Instead of being sent overseas, he was sent to Fort Bliss, Texas.

Straight out of service, Parsons initially applied for jobs as a wildlife biologist, but most of them required a master's degree. In 1972, Parsons applied and got accepted to the Wildlife Ecology Program at Oregon State University, where he studied the American dipper, North America's only aquatic songbird. For two winters Parsons spent the hours between sunup and sundown along Lookout Creek, a tributary of the Blue River, sitting behind a blind and watching dippers. "It was pretty cold and the conditions could be harsh," he says of the experience. "Sometimes it snowed and I went in on cross-country skis." He adds, "It was great fun observing the antics of those fascinating birds."

Once he completed his master's degree, Parsons worked in several government jobs as a biologist, first with the Army Corps of Engineers looking at the impact of dredging and dams on fish, wildlife, and riverine ecosystems, then with the United States Fish and Wildlife Service (FWS), where he held a variety of positions. It was perhaps his first job with the FWS, bringing people and agencies together to achieve consensus about management of the natural resources along the upper

Mississippi River, which prepared him best for the conflict and chaos of wolf politics that would come to define his career some twenty years later.

Parsons's second assignment took him to Cookeville, Tennessee, where he worked along the Obion-Forked Deer River system, which he calls "an ecologically rich, very appealing habitat, even if you're chest deep in water with water moccasins swimming around you." Because it naturally flooded several times a year, the Army Corps of Engineers wanted to channelize 225 miles of these rivers so their swampy floodplains could be drained and converted to agricultural uses—primarily soybean production. Parsons was assigned to evaluate the impacts of the project. The Environmental Defense Fund, joined by several other conservation groups, filed a suit against the Army Corps, saying their project violated the Clean Water Act.

Because of his expertise, Parsons was called to testify. His testimony lasted four hours and when he was done, Parsons says, "The judge turned to me and said, 'Mr. Parsons, I don't know if you've ever testified in a federal court before, but you are the best witness I've ever had in my witness chair.'" The environmental side won and Parsons says, "We saved about 100 thousand acres of riverside swamps and forests in the Obion-Forked Deer River Basin."

In 1990, after moving to Albuquerque for another job that Parsons calls "not that interesting and a placeholder [in his career]," a new job with the FWS was created and opened for applications. The job was to coordinate the recovery project for the endangered Mexican gray wolf, and Parsons knew it would be far more interesting and challenging than the job he was in. He tossed his name in the hat.

The reason there was even a need for a recovery effort for the Mexican wolf started over one hundred years ago when, towards the end of the nineteenth century, livestock owners dominated the extensive western grazing ranges. After a series of political battles, and with a congressional appropriation of $125,000 in 1915, the US Bureau of Biological Survey started slaughtering gray wolves. Then, in 1919, the federal government passed a law calling for a systematic extermination of all wolves on all federal lands.

By the 1970s, after the federal eradication policy to rid the land of predators and sanitize it for livestock, nearly all the gray wolves in the lower forty-eight states had been killed. Nobody knows exactly how many wolves were slaughtered, but it was likely in the hundreds of thousands. When *el lobo* was finally listed as endangered under the newly implemented Endangered Species Act in 1976, there was not a single Mexican wolf left on US soil. The last five survivors, found in Mexico, were trapped and bred in captivity with the hopes of someday being returned to the wild.

🐾

Two weeks before the FWS announced who had gotten the Mexican wolf recovery coordinator position, Parsons was hiking in the Gila wilderness in southwestern New Mexico—the world's first designated wilderness—with his best friend from his army days. "We were doing an epic backpacking trip of about eighty miles. We were sitting around a campfire in perfect wolf habitat, pondering the future and I said, 'Wouldn't it be cool if I got the job with the FWS and we came back here in ten years and heard wolves howl?'"

When Parsons got home from the trip, he found out he had gotten the job.

🐾

As the Mexican wolf recovery coordinator, Parsons's first task was to start the process of drafting an environmental impact statement (EIS) showing the feasibility of Mexican wolf recovery and answering such questions as whether reintroduction was feasible and where the wolves would be released to ensure their continued survival in the wild. Parsons admits that he was initially naïve about the difficulties he would face. "I knew the recovery would be a long process. I'd have to draft an environmental impact statement and related decision documents and regulations and hold public hearings at every step, all the while never knowing if a wolf would ever even get released."

And keeping those animals alive has been, if anything, a fight—one that Parsons fought on two fronts: a battle with government and a battle on the ground.

The battle with the government started when Parsons and his team bored into the data and it became clear that the best places to release the Mexican wolf were in the Apache and Gila National Forests in eastern Arizona and western New Mexico, collectively known as the Blue Range Wolf Recovery Area. "Yet the FWS forced us to add the White Sands Missile Range to the mix of possible release sites," he explains. Parsons's analysis revealed that White Sands, a four thousand-square-mile missile testing range, which includes a national monument of glistening sand and gypsum dunes in southern New Mexico, was not a place where wolves could survive in numbers needed to achieve recovery. Despite his analysis, Parsons says, "It became apparent that the FWS had made a backroom deal with Arizona, New Mexico, and Texas and their respective game commissioners that the initial releases would be at White Sands."

Twice Parsons was reminded in private conversations with his regional director, John Rogers, that regardless of the analysis presented in the EIS, the initial reintroduction would take place at White Sands. Parsons began to sense the rising political heat and knew that following this directive would violate the "best science" mandate of the Endangered Species Act and could lead to the lobos' extinction.

The ground battle took place in public hearings held throughout rural areas of Arizona, New Mexico, and Texas. The primary opponents to restoring Mexican wolves to their wild, native habitats were ranchers, local elected officials, and self-described "sportsmen." The latter two factions strongly sympathized with ranchers. Parsons was about to jump into a crash course on the political clout wielded by the ranching industry, which accounts for less than 1 percent of the population.

At one of the many public hearings presided over by Parsons, he was told by a man who testified that he'd hold Parsons responsible for the first person who gets killed by a wolf. "You're more likely to get hit by lightning than get killed by a wolf," explains Parsons. "There are 5,500 gray wolves right now in the lower forty-eight states, and not a single case of a human attack. In Catron County, New Mexico, they're so paranoid about wolves that they're building 'wolf-proof school bus shelters' for their kids, so they won't get eaten by wolves on their way to school." In other words, spreading fear not based on science or statistics is perpetuating the myth of the "big bad wolf."

Another meeting that stands out for Parsons was when, in the mid-1990s, he was invited to take part in a panel and explain the wolf reintroduction proposal at a meeting of the New Mexico Cattle Growers Association in Albuquerque. "I was the only one on the panel who was pro wolf," Parsons explains. "As I walked down the aisle to exit the hall after the panel discussion, a guy sitting next to the aisle stared at me with the most penetrating eye contact you can imagine and said, 'Someone's going to get killed over this deal.'"

And at a third meeting in Silver City, New Mexico, in 2000, when Parsons was testifying for the first time as a private citizen, things got violent:

> I turn away from the podium and a big cowboy in a big black hat named J. Zane Walley is standing in the way of my retreat and he turns to me and says, "I hate your f***ing ass." The guy is about six foot, three inches. There's a guy next to him, a shorter, stocky guy, also with a black hat, who looks at me and says, "Yeah, and he's not the only one." There's a little gap to move through, so I say, "I'm sorry you feel that way," and I walk through. A reporter from the *Phoenix New Times* moves in to see what's going on and Walley punches the reporter. I had walked away from it. It wasn't a fight I could win.

Despite the inflammatory comments and the conflict, Parsons has never considered giving up. "You just don't say anything. You move on," he says. "I don't take things personally. I'm just the messenger. In a different setting, those people might actually like me." Parsons also keeps fighting for the wolf because he understands the biological significance wolves play in a healthy ecosystem. In the Southwest, Mexican wolves and cougars are keystone species, top carnivores that maintain biological diversity in the ecosystem, improve habitat, and perform a number of other critical ecological roles. "People should understand that nature has a plan, and that all species evolved with a role to play," he says. "We don't know everything about nature, and we shouldn't be playing God."

An equally important early task for Parsons as Mexican wolf recovery coordinator was to start expanding the captive breeding program of those five original wolves brought in from Mexico. Because those wolves included only one female (pregnant when captured) and the only female pup in her first litter died, the captive breeding program got off to a very slow start. Fortunately, two other lineages of presumed

Mexican wolves existed in captivity elsewhere. "I asked a team of geneticists to analyze the genetic purity of the three populations of Mexican wolves living in captivity. All the lines turned out to be pure Mexican wolf (meaning they were not crossed with genes from dogs or coyotes). This gave us the green light to start merging the lines to capture the different gene variants," Parsons says, and then adds, "This was a big milestone for the recovery program."

It might have been a milestone, but while the human battle was being fought, most of those mixed-gene wolves, knowing nothing of humans and their politics, have withered away in captivity due to pressure from states on the FWS to limit their release. "Politics has wasted entire generations of the most genetically valuable wolves in captivity," Parsons says. Despite his frustration with the situation—both then and now—he says, "There are politics everywhere. You have to find a path through it. You can't fight it all. You have to decide what's worth fighting for or you'll burn out." He goes on to say, "Nothing happens if people don't care. If you don't advocate and go out of your way to support what you love, it won't be saved. We save what we love." For Parsons, that has meant twenty-six years of his life dedicated to saving the Mexican wolf—and still counting.

The reintroduction process limped along with more documents, more backroom deals, and more paperwork until Parsons was sent to Washington, DC, in 1997 to meet first with the acting director of the FWS, John Rogers (who had been Parsons's boss in New Mexico) and then with United States Secretary of the Interior, Bruce Babbitt. The meetings were about where to release the wolves—White Sands or Blue Range. Parsons recalls the pivotal experience, the moment that set the fate of Mexican wolves in motion. He had prepared his briefing, based on best available science, to recommend that the wolves be released in the Blue Range. Recalling the meeting, Parsons remembers:

> I get five words out and Rogers starts chewing my ass for not proposing the release in White Sands. He says we have the science that says White Sands can support sixty wolves. I'm like holy crap! What's happening here? My bosses are just sitting

there, watching me get berated by the agency director. I said, "John, we never had that science." John never let up. He never gave me his support. He had apparently made a commitment to White Sands behind closed doors, and I had caused him to lose face with his state counterparts. Then it was time to brief the Secretary of the Interior. Now I'm really fried. I'm a wreck. What am I supposed to say? I don't have the endorsement from Rogers and he's at the briefing along with about twenty other Interior officials. I just made a decision. I only came with one briefing and one recommendation. I'd give it to the Secretary.

Babbitt agreed with Parsons's science-supported recommendation and didn't bow to the politics of the states. As such, Parsons believes that without the eight-year window of political opportunity under the Clinton administration with Babbitt as Secretary of the Interior, there would be no more Mexican wolves today. He also credits the thousands of other people in dozens of different areas from the captive wolf management community to the staff and volunteers with the agencies to the scientists who conducted the relevant research, and perhaps most importantly, the dedicated citizen advocates who kept the drums beating in support of the lobos, all of whom worked tirelessly and none of whom can be overlooked. One could also say the same of Parsons: without his determination, perseverance, and emotional wherewithal, Mexican wolves would be a thing of the past.

🐾

In 1998, it was time to put wolves back into the wild. Eleven wolves from three different packs were released south of Alpine, Arizona, in the Apache National Forest. The Mexican wolf release was Parsons's exit ticket from the service, and in 1999 he retired. He might have retired from the service, but he didn't retire from wolves.

Then, in March 2000, it was time to put the wolves back into the Gila, a place Parsons deeply loves. He was asked by the field team to volunteer to come with them and be the person to get left behind for a week to follow the wolves' movements. Of course he agreed. After an all-day trip, in which a male and a female Mexican wolf with an established pair bond were packed into the wilderness on mules in specially designed aluminum panniers, the team reached the remote release site. "It was dusk when we got there," says Parsons. "We carried the boxes into the holding pen (a pen stocked with food and water, which the wolves can chew out of when they're ready) and with a long rope, tripped the lever that opens them. One wolf charged out. The other took its time."

That night the team camped a mile away near Lilley Park, and the next day everyone but Parsons left. He recalls what happened next:

> I'm alone with the wolves in one of my favorite places on the planet. I had telemetry (tracking) gear, and early that evening I got signals from the wolves in the direction of the pen, suggesting they had not yet chewed out. I'm in my camping chair, having a great time, communing with the wilderness. Then 100 yards away or less, I hear a wolf howl. There is no mistaking a wolf howl. It was the real deal. They were out— the first wolves to roam free in that place in fifty years or so. I looked as hard as I could through the near darkness, then at about thirty or forty yards I could just barely see the silhouette of a wolf walk past my camp and head off into the wild.

That one reward might have been enough for Parsons, but then, as he had dreamed about ten years earlier, he and the same army buddy returned to repeat that weeklong backpack in the Gila. While there, they experienced firsthand a positive result of Parsons's lifetime work: "In the early twilight, there was a howl right next to our camp. I popped up and looked. The wolf had to be close, but it was too dark to see it. Hearing a wolf howl is the next best thing to seeing one, and, in some ways, it was even better."

Ten years after Parsons backpacked into the Gila and imagined the return of the wolf, *el lobo* was back, and maybe the howl was its way of saying thank you to the man who made it possible.

🐾

Parsons's battle and the battle for the Mexican wolf is far from over. In 2015, there were 110 wild Mexican wolves in Arizona and New Mexico. At the beginning of 2016, there were ninety-seven. Their numbers continue to fluctuate as the states maintain their anti-wolf stance and the USFWS stalls in coming up with a feasible recovery plan that includes more Mexican wolves being released into more places in the wild. (Because all living Mexican wolves today are descended from just seven founders, new releases are desperately needed to bolster their poor genetic diversity.)

Parsons has received many awards for his work, including the New Mexico Chapter of the Wildlife Society's annual Professional Award (2000), the North American Wolf Conference's Alpha Award (2006), the Sky Island Alliance Mike Seidman Memorial Award (2008), and the Wilburforce Foundation award for Outstanding Conservation Leadership (2008).

Parsons continues to fight for the Mexican wolf. "I've spent seventeen years since my retirement trying to protect the Mexican wolves' right to exist. There are many people who want it to go extinct, but I'm still devoting my life to it," he says. As for retirement: "I've known people in retirement who say they're bored. My response is that the only way you can be bored is if you don't care about anything. I can't relate to waking up each morning, playing a couple rounds of golf and watching TV all evening because there's still work to be done and time is running out for the lobos of the Southwest."

There's still work to be done, and, fortunately, Dave Parsons is there to do it.

It's time to put *Little Red Riding Hood* to rest and redefine our notion of the wolf—not as a fearsome killer that preys upon small children and vulnerable grannies, but as a keystone species, integral to a healthy ecosystem. We still have a chance to save *el lobo*, still have a chance for future generations to hear the howl of the wolf in the wild.

It has to come down to one thing: more wolves, less politics.

For more information on Dave Parsons, please visit www.mexicanwolves.org and www.projectcoyote.org.

CHAPTER 14

• • •

Ian Craig: Peace Maker

"If there is peace for the people, there is peace for wildlife."

—Ian Craig

Ian Craig.

WHEN IAN CRAIG WAS A child growing up on a sixty-two-thousand-acre cattle ranch near Mt. Kenya, Samburu and Maasai tribesmen would sometimes slip onto the ranch and steal his family's cattle. "It was something they had always done against other tribes," says Craig, referring to the traditional practice of cattle rustling as a way to replace animals lost to drought or disease. Although there was occasional small-scale violence in the practice, loss of human life was rare.

Since those years in the 1960s, cattle rustling in northern Kenya has evolved from a way to replenish herd stock to something much more serious—and deadly. In this arid region of little infrastructure, frequent drought, and severe poverty, gangs of cattle rustlers armed with AK-47s imported on the black market from Somalia often kill members of opposing tribes as they go after their livestock. By the start of the twenty-first century, hundreds of Borana, Rendile, and Samburu pastoralists, who survive by roaming and grazing their cattle, had been killed. Much of the wildlife had also been wiped out—killed by cattle rustlers who saw wildlife as competition.

Ian Craig is slowly changing all this, helping to reduce the cycle of violence amongst tribes and against wildlife. Thanks to the Northern Rangeland Trust (NRT), Craig's innovative conservation model, groups of once warring pastoralists have embraced wildlife conservation and taken steps toward peace. They are now organizing land into private conservancies that are working to "conserve wildlife, transform lives, and bring peace."

Craig is shaping conservation in Kenya, just as Kenya shaped Craig.

🐾

Craig was born in 1952 in the town of Nanyuki to a Scottish mother, who had been born in Kenya, and an English father, who first came to Kenya while based with the British army. As a child with the Kenyan landscape as a playground, Craig was happiest when he was out walking in wild places with his good friend Kinyanjui Lesenteria, a Maasai man who worked on his parents' ranch in the late 1960s and '70s. "Kinyanjui had a lifetime of living with animals. I had the desire to learn more, so we walked together to fulfill this enthusiasm." In the big, untamed wilderness of northern Kenya, it was easy for the two to satisfy their interests, and they became friends. "We would go off exploring, sometimes for a week at a time, living out in the bush with wildlife. We built a close relationship. He taught me everything I know about wildlife and tracking."

Craig also shared another childhood passion with Kinyanjui: hunting. "As a child I was an avid hunter. I lived to track and hunt animals, not in numbers, but for the thrill of being close to wildlife in wild places. I would spend extended periods of time with Kinyanjui in the forests and the mountains."

After Craig was sent off to Ireland to live with his grandparents and finish his schooling, he returned to his beloved Kenya and spent several years working as a professional hunting guide. It was a poaching incident that he and Kinyanjui witnessed in May 1989 in Kenya's Matthews Mountains that served as the impetus for Craig to give up hunting for good and make him realize that he could personally influence whether or not there would be wildlife left in the future. "That day I watched eight poachers kill six elephants and cut out their ivory," he says. "I was with Kinyanjui when we saw the poachers. We didn't have suitable firearms for any sort of confrontation, and so we had to stay hidden for safety and watch the whole scene over a twenty-four-hour period from the animals being shot to their ivory being cut out and hidden."

Although Craig gave up hunting after the incident, turning his life toward conservation, he believes his years as a hunter helped him better understand wildlife. "I understand animals in a different way than scientists understand them," he says. "My days and passion for hunting were the foundation for my conservation career. Having hunted animals, the transition to conserving them was a relatively obvious progression, and I see my time hunting as training for what I do now. Hunting brought me close to wild animals and wild places and gave me the realization that they are both disappearing before our eyes and yet we can do something about it."

In 1978 Craig moved back to his family cattle ranch, which had been in the family since 1924, and he was put in charge of its operations. His parents were unusual for ranchers. They did not disdain wildlife as competition for their cattle. Instead, they valued it. The Craig family motto was to leave room for wildlife, so much so that in 1983 when a family friend suggested that they establish a protected part of their land for white and black rhinos—animals whose populations, due to poaching, had dropped dramatically from twenty thousand in 1960 to less than five hundred in 1983—the Craigs eagerly agreed. They fenced and protected 4,900 acres of their land for a rhino sanctuary. After ten years of success with the rhinos, which resulted in a large population increase, the Craigs expanded the sanctuary to cover the rest of the ranch as well as the adjoining Ngare Ndare Forest Reserve. That sanctuary evolved into the Lewa Wildlife Conservancy that today is home to some of Africa's most endangered species, including not just the rhino, but also Grevy's zebra, reticulated giraffe, and sitatunga, a shy, aquatic antelope.

Lewa, however, wasn't enough to keep the animals protected. Although the perimeter of the conservancy was almost entirely fenced, corridors for animal movement needed to be maintained. Lewa achieved that goal of connecting their private land and neighboring wildlife areas by leaving gaps in the fences. This meant that when animals left Lewa, they were often butchered for meat or ivory. "It became clear that Lewa's wildlife would only flourish with help from the surrounding communities," says Craig.

In 1993, wondering how to best gain the help, the trust, and the support of the surrounding tribal areas, Craig turned to Peter Jenkins, one of Kenya's most famous colonial game wardens in the Meru and Tsavo National Parks from 1944 to 1979—and also one of Craig's mentors. "Jenkins said to me, let's spend three weeks in South Africa and see what they're doing to protect their wildlife," recalls Craig. "Jenkins was so respected we were able to go there and meet with top government people."

South Africa's model of small, fenced reserves based on hunting was a success, but Craig and Jenkins knew that threats to wildlife, such as cattle rustling, were different in Kenya. There, they'd need a new style of conservation, a style that didn't exclude local people, but rather embraced them. Craig started to seriously consider a holistic approach to conservation, one in which land isn't owned or fenced. He wanted an approach that would address the root causes of human-animal conflict—a lack of peace and prosperity among the communities that coinhabit the land—and that would bring people together to do business. "Business," says Craig, "is good for conservation." This approach became known as the conservancy model. But as Craig soon learned, thinking about conservancies was one thing; starting them was another altogether.

In the early 1990s, Craig wanted to set up the first conservancy in Il Ngwesi on the north border of Lewa, but the Maasai who lived there weren't keen on the idea. In fact, they thought the conservancy was a trick to take away their land and turn it into a national park or a wildlife sanctuary, a form of the old-school management practices that left local people out of the equation. "In these pastoralist societies, trust is massively important," says Craig. "It takes a long time to build up trust. If communities don't trust us, we could achieve nothing." Craig's old friend Kinyanjui was instrumental in helping Craig gain that trust. "Kinyanjui was my bridge into the communities," explains Craig. "He was instrumental in brokering deals."

Craig and Kinyanjui took Maasai elders of the area to visit Lewa and the famous Maasai Mara Park in southern Kenya to see how wildlife tourism could become part of generating income. Through several years of collaboration, sharing, hard work, patience, and commitment (it doesn't hurt that he speaks fluent Swahili and understands the cattle business), Craig gained the trust of the Maasai. In 1995, Il Ngwesi became the first conservancy. The Il Ngwesi Community Trust, a twenty-three-thousand-acre area with a community safari lodge, created thirty-six permanent jobs, including rangers and administrative positions. With better land management practices and restored grassland productivity, wildlife rebounded.

Today Il Ngwesi is just one of nineteen conservancies supported by NRT. Now Lewa sits at the southern tip of a contiguous corridor of conservancies covering more than five million acres that are home to 212,000 people, as well as increasing numbers of endangered rhinos, elephants, and antelope. NRT, with the guidance of a thirty-member tribal council of elders, helps these conservancies by providing funds, management support, and a wide range of trainings without sacrificing each conservancy's independence.

If there is one phrase that perhaps best summarizes NRT, it is a quote by the honorable Francis Ole Kaparo, cofounder of NRT and chairman of its board of trustees, which is found in the foreword to *The Story of the Northern Rangelands Trust* brochure: "Conservation for the people by the people." Working with NRT, the conservancies channel the proceeds that are gained through ecotourism, cattle sales (which NRT helps broker, thus alleviating cattle rustling), and other income-generating projects into education and development projects such as building schools and health clinics that the community decides on. "Conservancies provide long-term employment to local people. They give them a cohesive voice, a democratic company to help them do business with the government, with non-governmental organization investors, with livestock marketing and mining companies, with any business," says Craig. "They can also sell their livestock into the NRT livestock market where it fetches a better price than families would've otherwise received. Forming a conservancy will also bring peace," he says. "Northern Kenya is plagued with ethnic divisions and illegal firearms, and this has helped build a forum for neighbors to talk to each other about stealing cattle. That peace is probably our biggest success from a community perspective."

Conservancies are not only good for people, they're good for wild-life as well. For example, in 1973 there were 160,000 elephants in Kenya. By 1993, there were fewer than twenty thousand. The population is now estimated to be at about thirty-two thousand. And elephants are not the only animals to have benefited. In the conservancies the numbers of Grevy's zebra, rhino, giraffe, cheetah, hirola antelope (which are be-ing brought back from the brink of extinction in the Ishaqbini Hirola Conservancy), and oryx have gone up. "Our worst year of poaching was in 2012 when we lost 138 elephants," says Craig. "In 2015, we only lost eighteen. Communities have really stepped up to stop poaching. When poaching goes down, income goes up," he adds, discussing the Sera Conservancy, a top income generator in ecotourism. "Recently I signed a check for scholarships for 648 children to go to school, proving that from tourism comes revenue. That, to me, is success—when poaching is down and revenue is up. Governments have endorsed the work and communities are leading it."

🐾

To protect elephants and rhinos from poachers, NRT has two dedi-cated anti-poaching teams that are working closely with the Kenyan Wildlife Services and conservancy rangers. Additionally, NRT has sent more than three hundred of the community conservancy rangers to the Kenya Wildlife Service Field Training Schools. Many of these rangers have become certified Kenya police reservists, able to disarm poachers and make arrests.

The most powerful weapon against poaching, though, is still the community and their sense of ownership over their land and the animals that inhabit it. "People used to think all the wildlife belonged to the government," says Craig, "but now they see it as theirs. They care what happens." He goes on to explain:

Poachers are criminal. If you wanted to kill a rhino in Lewa, you would have to have inside knowledge and bribe some-one in the system to work with you. Even in the conservan-cies, there are criminals and people happy if there is enough money involved to kill a rhino inside the sanctuary. So you have a broker who bribes someone in the conservancy to kill a rhino. It's a local chain of events. To stop the poaching, we have a very sophisticated intelligence network here working with the government. We have a depository of all the bad people. The community knows the bad people. They will tell us if a person is looking to kill a rhino, so we start watching that person. That is what has reduced the poaching. There are great reasons why people would turn in poachers and support conservation. Most of the poachers have inside information and are locally known. The communities are now naming and shaming the poachers.

Poaching is reduced, but that doesn't mean poachers aren't still a danger; this is why Craig always carries a gun. "You can't do what I do without being shot at. It's par for the course," he says. "In a good year, I'm only shot at one or two times. In a bad year it's more like four or five times. I don't chase poachers anymore. I don't fly on poaching incidents. The poachers are quite happy to shoot at aircraft." He also says, "I would go to the end of the earth to get the person who killed an elephant, and I've built a network of individuals (including his wife, Jane) who feel the same way."

Through hunting and a lifetime of living with wildlife, Craig has learned much about animals. "Every animal is an individual just like people," he says. "They have character. They laugh. They play. They love and have emotions within their own society. In working with animals I take this fact into account in all my thinking."

Loving wildlife and working to protect it, though, is not without risk. Not just risk from poachers, but also from the animals themselves. Craig recognizes and accepts these hazards. "My most dangerous work has probably been darting rhino on foot (for sedation and relocation) before we had access to helicopters," he says. (A rhino that awakens from sedation will charge the first thing in sight.) Craig also recalls the time he nearly got killed by a leopard ("it chewed up my head and arm quite badly") and the time he was charged by a 1,300-pound Cape buffalo, an animal that has more than four times the strength of an ox and can easily tip a truck. "I was out in the open with no trees and no defense," he says. "I couldn't get my revolver, which I carry all the time. I ran straight at it and shouted and it finally stopped, five paces from me. By then I had grabbed my revolver and so I fired a shot in the air and the buffalo ran off. Otherwise I would be dead."

These near misses are the risks Craig is willing to accept in service of the larger goal to protect wildlife and help secure peace in his beloved Kenya. "Giving up hope isn't even a concept for me," he says. "I only wish I had started my conservation career working with communities twenty years earlier when there were still plenty of rhinos to conserve."

Despite wishing he had started earlier, Craig has a lot to celebrate and many reasons to be optimistic. Although Peter Jenkins taught him that "Working in conservation one needs to have a long-term view with every action and plan having a long time horizon," Craig has seen the pay-off of his hard work in a relatively short time. "I live in a very positive bubble because we have changed people's lives, and we've changed the future of wildlife," he says. "It's palpable. You can touch the success. No one in their wildest dreams would have thought there would be rhino going back into northern Kenya."

Craig and the communities he works with aren't the only ones recognizing NRT's accomplishments. In 2016, Craig's efforts were recognized by Queen Elizabeth II when he received the Officer of the Order of the British Empire (OBE) award in the Queen's Birthday Honor's List. The OBE recognizes distinguished service to the arts and sciences, public services outside the Civil Service, and work with charitable and welfare organizations of all kinds. Craig's Lewa Wildlife Conservancy is also internationally renowned as a United Nations Educational, Scientific, and Cultural Organization (UNESCO) World Heritage Site. (UNESCO identifies, protects, and preserves places of cultural and natural heritage around the world that are considered to be of outstanding value to humanity.) Lewa is also featured on the International Union for the Conservation of Nature's Green List, a list that "celebrates protected area success, acting as a benchmark for progress towards effective and equitable management and rewarding innovation, excellence, and enterprise."

Reflecting on his successes, Craig offers this advice to people who, like him, want to find real a way to make a contribution to conservation: "Find tangible engagement in a real-time situation. Working in conservation is about commitment, a certain amount of dreaming with high ambitions and making those a reality." He hopes he has passed this long-term commitment to the person he calls his closest and most special friend: his granddaughter.

Wildlife conservation in Kenya is no longer a case of "them or us"—the "them" in this case meaning wildlife—mentality. Wildlife instead is a beacon of hope. The NRT model of conservancies is a model that can be replicated anywhere in the world where there is communal ownership of a land asset. Craig has shown that across the globe it's possible to bring together the needs of local people with the protection of wildlife. "Suddenly people's children have clothes and can go to school. That's the role of NRT. Why should the world invest in animals such as the Sarias rhino and others like them? Because it brings peace."

Simply put, if it's good for people, it's good for wildlife. That is the model Craig is bringing daily to the world.

For more information on Ian Craig, please visit www.nrt-kenya.org.

CHAPTER 15

• • •

Megan Parker, PhD:
Canines and Conservation

"Animals are so much more sentient and able to communicate
than humans give them credit for."

—Dr. Megan Parker

Megan Parker with Pepin.

MEGAN PARKER LIKES BAD DOGS—THE obsessive kind that won't stop bringing you a slobbery ball to throw. Of the approximately one million dogs euthanized in shelters across the country each year, Parker and her partners at Working Dogs for Conservation (WD4C) rescue rare handfuls of those high-energy, driven dogs that few others want. These dogs don't just get rescued; they get to work, putting their special skills to use in an array of conservation-related activities. From sniffing

139

out firearms and ammunition used by poachers in Zambia, to detecting invasive weeds before they break the surface in Montana, these dogs become heroes that would otherwise have been killed, but for Parker's efforts.

❧

Parker grew up in Missoula, Montana, as the youngest of four children in a pro-conservation family. She calls her childhood idyllic, recalling weekends spent in a remote cabin on a lake south of Glacier National Park. "We had to canoe across the lake to get to the house," she says. "And my family did a lot of backpacking and hiking and river trips." It wasn't just the idyllic times in the outdoors that were a constant for her; it was animals too.

Both her father and grandfather loved and raised dogs, igniting Parker's interest in canines at a young age. "When I was ten, my dad traveled all over Montana with me going to different kennels, helping me to pick out the right dog," says Parker. "We'd talk to different breeders and I got to know about all different kinds of dogs." After she settled on the right dog, a Shetland sheepdog she named Brandy, her father got the pair enrolled in obedience classes, so Parker could train Brandy herself. Besides Brandy, Parker and her family had a variety of other dogs and breeds, from dachshunds to German shepherds to St. Bernards.

It wasn't just domestic animals that she got to know, but wild ones too. Parker's family was friends with the famous biologist John Craighead, who worked at the university with her dad in Missoula. "He gave us a baby owl, and he had hawks and eagles. I spent days and days watching them," recalls Parker. "From my first memories, I had pets to love and an appreciation of wildlife."

This appreciation of wildlife led Parker to study art and biology at Middlebury College in Vermont. After graduation, she moved to New York City, where she worked in a veterinary clinic while attending Columbia University to earn a post-baccalaureate degree in pre-med with a focus on veterinary medicine. Her time in veterinary clinics taught her something important. "While I loved the medicine, I realized that I wasn't suited for the business aspect of having a clinic," she says. What she was more suited for was a life that drew on her childhood, a life in the outdoors where she could be in the field. With this in mind,

Parker went back to graduate school at Boise State University and earned a master's in raptor ecology. She worked for the Peregrine Fund, studying bat falcons and laughing falcons at Mayan ruins in the rainforests of Tikal National Park in Guatemala.

Although her thesis was on falcons, Parker's focus soon turned to wolves. "I was living in Idaho, writing up my dissertation, and there was a captive wolf project in the Stanley Basin," she says. "The woman who was caretaking the wolves was leaving and I stepped into her job at the Wolf Education and Research Center in Stanley and Winchester, Idaho." Parker was a researcher, so when the reintroduction of wolves into Idaho and Yellowstone was gearing up in 1995, she got to be part of the Idaho reintroduction team. Half of the wolves in the reintroduction went to Idaho and half to Yellowstone. The Yellowstone wolves were a soft release, meaning they first went into pens before being set free. The Idaho population was a hard release, sending the wolves directly from Canada, where they'd been captured, into the Idaho wilderness. "It was a grand experiment," says Parker. "But biologically it worked, meaning the wolves thrived in both areas."

Through working in wolf introduction, Parker got her start in training dogs for conservation. Specifically, a call from a biologist, who was wondering if dogs could be used to locate wolf scat, prompted Parker's curiosity. "I called a lot of police dog trainers and detection dog trainers to see if they could help me train a dog to sniff out wolf scat. (Scat is used to determine presence of a species in an area and also to collect information about their DNA, hormones, diet, and how they use the landscape, as well as to conduct population counts. Detection, or sniffer, dogs are those canines trained to detect substances such as explosives, illegal drugs, currency, or blood.) Most of them laughed at my idea, but I talked to a friend of mine who was a police chief in New York and he gave me the name of Barbara Davenport, a detection dog trainer for the Department of Corrections in Washington state. She was willing to take a risk with my crazy request."

Davenport enabled Parker to get the necessary government clearance and head to an island off of Tacoma, Washington to learn how she trained the dogs. After Parker learned Davenport's techniques, the two searched for a method to turn the skills of sniffing for drugs into sniffing for scat. Although field biologists had been working with dogs before this time, there had been no formal protocol for how to train the animals to do such work. "This was the first formal, systematic attempt to teach dogs to find scats. Davenport was great," says Parker. "She took a risk in training biologists to train dogs."

After developing the training protocols, Parker wanted to put their work to the test with Dr. Sam Wasser, who was studying bears in Washington. Together with Aimee Hurt, the two spent a summer around the Okanogan Valley in Washington, conducting a population study on bears. To conduct the study, they used Finney and Dharma, two black lab rescues that had been trained to sniff for bear scat. "We wanted to know how dogs would actually do in the field. Could they find the bear scat?" The dogs did beautifully—finding the scat, doing what was asked of them, working tirelessly.

Parker and Hurt then teamed up with Deborah Woollett and Alice Whitelaw, both dog handlers and biologists, to see how else they could use dogs for conservation. Could they use dogs to increase hard-to-find and rare sample sizes? How about to gather data non-invasively? Or to find invasive weeds? What about fish? Ammunition? Ivory?

Dogs, it turns out, could do all of these things, and do them well.

In all dogs, their sense of smell is far more developed than humans can even imagine. For example, WD4C dogs have detected scat from a distance of 550 yards. They have found scat of target species under water in a flooded stream. They have sniffed out a penny-sized percussion cap used to fire an illegal weapon that was hidden in a packed suitcase in a jam-packed bus in Africa.

A dog's astounding ability to detect odors comes from several factors. Dogs have up to 300 million olfactory receptors in their noses, compared to about five million in humans, and a much larger part of their brain is devoted to analyzing smell. Additionally, dogs' noses work differently than human noses. When humans inhale, we smell and breathe through the same airway. When a dog inhales, a fold of tissue just inside their nostril helps to separate the two functions of smelling and respiration. Further enabling their olfactory ability is the mechanics of how a dog exhales, which allows it to sniff more or less continuously. They can also wiggle each nostril independently—making them able to determine through which nostril they detect an odor. Finally, dogs have an organ that humans lack: the Jacobson's organ, which picks up pheromones, chemicals that are unique to each animal and that provide a host of olfactory information about their sexual status.

But it's not just a good nose that makes a dog an ideal partner for conservation work; it's also behavior. "Working dogs such as shepherds, collies, and labs have been selected to work with people and to 'tell' people what they know," explains Parker. But selecting a dog isn't breed specific. Parker and her colleagues choose dogs with an over-the-top desire to play with a toy. "The ones we choose are high speed, hell to live with, high energy, and obsessive-compulsive. They will do anything to fetch or tug." To train the dogs, Parker links the scent of whatever target she's training the dog on, be it ivory, ammunition, or invasive weeds, with a reward, usually a ball or a tug toy. "All of our training is positive. We link what they love with what we want them to find."

Then there's personality. "A dog that's very deliberate, careful, and methodical will be good for a task with live animals; as opposed to my dog, Pepin, a Belgian Malinois who has a high prey drive and likes to chase stuff," Parker says. "He wouldn't be good on a black footed ferret project, for example." You don't want your dogs to scare, touch, hurt— or eat—their target. "We never use bird dogs. If a duck flies overhead, we don't want our dogs to be distracted. They have to know that when they're working they're completely focused on what we're asking them to find and that they won't chase after livestock or wildlife. The dogs have to be able to give 100 percent while they're working." When they find and train the right dog, Parker says, "The dog loves it. When it loves what it's doing and has focus and drive, we keep it busy."

And it's not just that a dog has stamina or can run that makes it a good candidate. "I can take my dog for a ten-mile run and then he comes home and wants to chase a ball. They need mental stimulation. These dogs are made to do this. They love their work," says Parker.

Understandably, it's not every day WD4C finds a dog that meets all of these criteria. Figuring out a dog's distractibility in various environments is part of the screening process before WD4C commits to training them. "A lot of dogs fail out during training," says Parker. "If the dog decides this isn't for them, we find them a high-energy forever home." In order to locate potential dogs nationally in the United States, WD4C has partnered with the International Fund for Animal Welfare (IFAW) to create the Rescues2theRescue program, which uses online tools to teach staff at animal shelters how to identify dogs that would be good candidates. Each year, Rescues2theRescue helps to save shelter, stranded, and death row canines by putting them to work for dog organizations around the world.

🐾

After Parker started working with Woollett, Whitelaw, and Hurt, she decided the best thing she could do for the organization, which they officially named Working Dogs for Conservation in 2000, was to return to school and to get a PhD. "I realized a PhD would help us to apply for grants and to do our own research," says Parker, so while working with WD4C, she entered a doctoral program in wildlife biology at the University of Montana in Missoula. Her research and dissertation on the scent marking behavior and territoriality of wild dogs in Botswana led her to Africa, so she was often away from the organization. As soon as she finished her dissertation, however, she went straight back to work. "By that time my partners had built the organization into something more stable and the field itself had grown into something bigger," she says.

The scope of what WD4C does and has accomplished has continued to grow since 2000, and every year more biologists working in universities, international NGOs, state and federal agencies, and private industry have been requesting their dogs. It's not just training that Parker and WD4C does, though. They provide everything from study design and methodology development to proposal writing, data collection, GIS (geographic information system) mapping, data analysis, and reporting. And they each work their own trained dogs.

Parker's dog, Pepin, was adopted from a breeder in Holland. He is specifically trained to detect over twenty scents, including snow leopard, wolverine, snares, and cheetah. On the WD4C website, Pepin's bio says: "Pepin has two speeds, 0 and 11. When he is at 11, his scenting skills verge on magical."

One of Pepin's many jobs has been a pilot project to detect invasive brook trout in adversely affected ecosystems and fisheries across the west. Another job he has had is helping to eradicate the invasive weed Dryer's woad (*lsatis tinctorial*) from the grasslands of Mount Sentinel in Missoula.

With a single plant able to produce as many as ten thousand seeds, Dyer's woad chokes out native grasslands habitat. For fifteen years, humans worked to eradicate the weed, but their efforts had little effect. In

2011, the University of Montana, Montana State University, the city of Missoula, the Missoula County Weed District, and the Montana Native Plant Society teamed up with WD4C to try a new approach. "Our detection dogs were able to locate Dyer's woad at all reproductive stages, especially those that people can't see," Parker explains. Thanks to the work of WD4C dogs, Dyer's woad has been beaten back by 99.8 percent. Parker believes that finding invasive weeds is one of the more amazing things the dogs do. "As humans we just see a sea of green plants that all look similar. That dogs can identify a tiny sprout of an invasive species is incredible."

Pepin has also been an ambassador for his species. In studying whether they could use dogs to help count elephants, Parker and Hurt flew with their dogs, Pepin and Wicket, to Myanmar. "Dogs are not kept as pets in Myanmar," Parker says, so whenever she was out with Pepin masses of children would come to stare. They were scared, so she started playing ball with Pepin. The kids gathered closer, but they would run away every time he walked up to them. "Then one brave kid was dared to touch the dog," she says. That child's feat echoed throughout the group of children until there were about 150 kids crammed around Pepin. Pepin let them all touch him without any complaint. "We ask so much of these dogs," Parker says. "They fly for hours, are crammed in the car and driven for miles, put on the tops of elephants, asked to swim across rivers. And they are always ready to work."

Parker has trained many other dogs besides Pepin. She and her colleagues train dogs that get placed in countries as far away as Zambia, where there are currently five dogs stationed in the South and North Luangwa Valley—Ruger, Chai, Earl, Sara, and Vicka. Collectively these dogs are trained to detect pangolin scales, leopard skins, lion, mokula lumber, gunpowder, elephant ivory, rhino horn, illegal ammunition, and illegal bush meat species. Ruger, a Labrador retriever–German shepherd mix who came off the Blackfeet reservation in Montana, was one of the first trained anti-poaching dogs there.

🐾

In 2014, Ruger started working with the scouts of the "Delta Team," a Zambian conservation law enforcement unit. Because pet dogs are not common in Zambia and most people are afraid of them, the scouts were at first skeptical about partnering with a canine. "Most local people in Zambia are used to throwing rocks at dogs to keep them away, so it's quite a leap to get them to make the mental shift that a dog can be a colleague," says Parker. "We help scouts make the shift through embarrassing training exercises that include talking in high, soft voices that are more appealing to dogs and having the scouts sit with the dogs to learn how they move and behave. It just takes a month for the scouts to develop a strong bond and to have the handling skills to work with a dog. It's a gratifying progression to watch them being trained. The scouts come to think of their dogs as colleagues."

And they are.

On Ruger's first mission, he accompanied the scouts to a location where a roadblock had been set up to search cars that might be carrying illegal goods. Ruger could search a car in three to four minutes, a job that would take humans hours. During the search of one car, Ruger sat and stared at a scout—his signal that he'd smelled something. When the scouts searched through several pieces of luggage and found nothing, they were discouraged, wondering if Ruger was actually up for this task. Ruger did not give up. He kept starting at one piece of luggage. Eventually the scouts found a matchbox wrapped in a plastic bag that held a primer cap—an illegal firing pin for a handmade rifle. At this moment, Ruger became more than a just dog; he became a partner.

Since then Ruger has been responsible for dozens of arrests for illegal wildlife products and illegal ammunition, and he has put about 150 poachers out of business by taking guns out of their hands. All of this accomplished by a dog who's going blind. The lack of vision, however, doesn't stop him. If anything, it makes him better at what he does, as he stays entirely focused on his sense of smell.

WD4C dogs are involved in dozens of projects. They assist in determining habitat selection and movement patterns of bears, mountain lions, and wolves in Idaho and Montana. They are working at customs ports in Kyrgyzstan, detecting illegal wildlife traffic. The dogs work at detecting invasive zebra and quagga mussels in both their microscopic larval stage, which humans can't see with a naked eye, and their adult stage in places such as Montana and Alberta, Canada. They're helping stop the spread of the emerald ash borer, an infestation that has killed millions of trees in the forests of Minnesota, and near Yellowstone they're testing to see if the dogs can sniff out the presence of the bacterial disease Brucellosis in free-ranging wildlife populations. These projects are just the beginning; the scope of what they do is constantly expanding.

For Parker, dogs are more than tools to aid in conservation; they're her life. "Even when I'm not working with dogs, I'm feeding them and taking care of them," she says, referring not just to Pepin, but to her three family dogs, as well as to the influx of new dogs she finds and trains—work she calls inspirational.

It's not just training dogs that inspires Parker, it's what the dogs accomplish as well. While working with dogs to prevent poaching, Parker has seen her share of "gut wrenching" wildlife kills. "But seeing the results the scouts and the dogs get and the number of guns they can take out of circulation is amazing," she says. "We work in impoverished areas where many people share a gun, so when you take one gun out of circulation, you're affecting a huge number of poachers and saving a lot of wildlife."

The interconnection of ecological systems and how little humans understand about the natural world are also sources of both inspiration and wonder for Parker. "The more we learn, the more I realize how complicated and interwoven everything is. Like how much a dog picks up from us when we're stressed and pumping stress hormones into the environment. Animals are so much more sentient and able to communicate than humans give them credit for."

Of Parker's many accomplishments, she is most proud of one closest to home: instilling awareness and a love of animals into her son. "He's so into conservation and nature and loves every aspect of it," she says. "He comes to Africa with me quite a bit. He thinks a lot about how to conserve wildlife and how to be in nature and how to live simply and how people used to live and survive."

As she's taught her son to think about conserving wildlife, she hopes others will do the same. "If you have a minute, sit still and look out the window to bring yourself closer to nature," she says. "Actions flow from appreciation. Every little thing helps. Turn off a light when you leave a room, recycle a piece of paper, give money to an organization you care about. It's going to take us all giving a little bit of time."

Humans might give a little bit of time, but WD4C dogs give everything, and in return they get solid retirement packages. After years of helping conservationists across the globe, each WD4C dog gets a forever home—and an abundance of balls to chase.

For more information on Meg Parker, please visit www.WD4C.org.

CHAPTER 16

• • •

Farwiza Farhan: Fighting for the Leuser Ecosystem

"I imagine a world where people's relationships with nature are at a level where the environment doesn't need 'protecting' because it will be the default position. This might sound utopic, but once upon a time abolition of slavery was utopic as well."

—Farwiza Farhan

Farwiza Farhan.

T HE ACEH PROVINCE ON THE northern tip of the Indonesian island of Sumatra, best—and most infamously—known throughout the world as the site of the catastrophic 2004 tsunami, has a reason to be recognized outside the realm of natural disaster. It is the home of the Leuser Ecosystem, an area of over six million acres of lowland rainforests, cloud forests, peat swamps, and alpine meadows, and is the last place on earth where orangutans, elephants, rhinos, and tigers coexist in the wild. The Leuser Ecosystem is one of the ecologically richest expanses of tropical rainforest found anywhere on the planet. It is also one of the most endangered.

🐾

Born in 1986, Farwiza Farhan grew up in the town of Banda Aceh in the Aceh province, living close to nature. Her childhood included idyllic pastimes such as swimming in the Batee Iliiek, a river near her grandmother's home, running wild on the beach with her (then) two sisters, climbing trees, and playing in the dirt with her friends. She wasn't allowed to watch television, except for harmless children's cartoons and nature documentaries, although she did manage to secretly turn on the TV when her parents were not home. "My parents were strong on installing grit and discipline, on school nights we weren't allowed to watch TV unless we could bear the boring evening news, and we could only watch for a few hours on the weekend," she says. More than any direct encounter with nature, though, it was through watching documentaries that Farwiza first grew amazed and curious about nature, ecosystems, and wildlife. "I watched BBC's *Blue Planet* over and over, imagining myself being in the ocean, looking at coral reefs, or out in the open water." That curiosity and interest led Farwiza to try out diving, hiking, and photography—activities that, she says, "brought me closer to the magical world that is around us."

For many girls in Farwiza's province, these interests might have been thwarted before they even had a chance to blossom. "Girls are encouraged to go to university and obtain higher education, but not to be overly ambitious in pursuing their career as it would make them un-marry-able," she says. "Following your passion is also discouraged, as many parents direct their children to pursue medical or engineering degrees, so they'll be able to make money once they graduate." For Farwiza, it was different. "My parents encouraged me to pursue my dreams. My father equipped us with education and independence. Their advice from the very beginning has always been, 'Do whatever you want to do, but be the best in whatever it is, follow it through with belief and passion, and live life with purpose.'"

As Farwiza watched nature documentaries and explored the outdoors, all the while contemplating her purpose, she started seriously thinking about conservation. "I grew up in a time and place where taking your rubbish out of your bin, then throwing it into the bush, the river, or the ocean was a normal thing," she says. "When I was ten years old, I had this dream that one day I'd have a small botanic garden with plants from all around the world packed into a few square meters of land. I started experimenting with fruit seeds I found in the kitchen, planting them in random places, feeding them with compost. This love slowly grew into a consciousness. I became more aware and mindful about waste disposal, and slowly educated myself on environmental issues. Over time I realized there was a lot more I could do to protect the environment."

In 2003, at age seventeen, Farwiza decided she would indeed follow her dream and passion to study environmental issues, in particular the ocean, and she enrolled to pursue a bachelor's degree in marine biology from University Sains Malaysia, Penang.

While at university, her undergraduate research supervisor, Professor Zulfigar Yasin, taught Farwiza the value of discipline and at the same time doing what you love. "He showed me that it's rewarding to be enjoying your work, no matter the long hours or the hard conditions," she says. "He had fun teaching and doing research and that happiness was infectious. He trusted me with projects I didn't think I could handle, while guiding and mentoring me along the way. I made lots of mistakes while I was doing my research and working for Prof. Zul, and he scolded me sometimes, but he made me believe that I could do things I previously had no confidence to do."

Returning home from Malaysia with a university degree in 2007, Farwiza had hardly any work experience, yet she was filled with pride and confidence, which she says bordered on arrogance. "I thought I could get any job I wanted. I couldn't have been more wrong," she says. "I walked into the office of a prominent environmental NGO with my CV in hand 'demanding' a job. Although the office didn't have any open vacancies, I insisted on applying. Unsurprisingly, I got rejected."

In 2009, Farwiza decided that in order to get the jobs she wanted, she needed to get more qualifications, so she took her education a step further and travelled to Queensland, Australia, for a master's degree in environmental management. In speaking about her time there, Farwiza says, "Studying at University of Queensland (UQ) was perhaps one of the turning points in my life. I learned to filter information and think critically, to evaluate my own thoughts and beliefs, and to value hard work. I made friends with people around the world whose perspective on life, education, and work ethics continue to stick with me until today." (As of 2016, she is pursuing her PhD at Radbound University Nijmegen in the Netherlands.)

Before she finished her master's degree, Farwiza was looking for a summer internship opportunity and her father introduced her to Mike Griffiths, a former oil company executive turned conservationist. At that time, Mike was working with Fauzan Azima, the chair of Leuser Ecosystem Management Authority, or BPKEL, and he offered her an internship. Although Farwiza did not end up interning with BPKEL at the time, she kept her relationship with Mike, and when she graduated UQ in 2010, he offered her a job to join the team. She accepted.

On her first day of the job Mike took Farwiza and a donor representative to see the Leuser Ecosystem first hand. "I instantly fell in love," she says, and goes on to describe the experience:

We flew over in a small plane and from above, as far as the eye could see, there was continuous forest, covered with patches of clouds. When we got there, we had a "small" hike of four hours just behind the research station. We saw a mother and baby orangutan, actually quite close. The forest is so dense and there is never a guarantee to see wild animals, so I felt so very lucky and honored. They swung down from a tree right near us before swinging away. The mother observed us for a moment before she decided to take off. They are so human-like. It made me wonder what could possibly go on in their minds? Were they analyzing or assessing how dangerous we could be? Were they merely trying to recognize these new faces that they never saw before? I don't know. But, in that short time, I got to witness the beauty of the Leuser Ecosystem and instantly felt inspired to participate in the effort to protect it.

Farwiza worked at BPKEL until 2012, when the newly elected government dissolved the organization, and the staff found themselves unemployed without warning or compensation. They were committed to the Leuser Ecosystem and its protection, though, so they decided to form a new organization and started Yayasan Hutan, Alam dan Ling-kungan Aceh (Forest, Nature and Environment Aceh Foundation), also known as HAkA, focused on protection, conservation, and restoration. The team elected Farwiza as the chairperson, trusting her to lead the organization forward. "Being chairperson is like being a captain of a ship," she says. "You don't necessarily know all the details, but you're supposed to see the big picture of where you're heading." She admits that sometimes being a young woman in a male-dominated environ-ment can be intimidating, and says she has faced numerous pressures from male opponents who try to force her to back down, which can feel uncomfortable. "But I draw strength from the support of my team and I don't worry so much about it," she says. "When things are heated in a meeting and I am under a lot of pressure, I try to just focus on getting my work done."

When she was a student pursuing her degree, Farwiza imagined that being a marine biologist or a conservationist would mean she would get to be in the field a lot and "have very little homework." Her expecta-tions couldn't have been further from the truth. "As much as happening in the field, conservation work also takes place in meeting rooms, on policy papers, on regulatory framework, in court," she says. The reality of the work, though, does not bother Farwiza; if anything, it inspires her:

> Conservation work could seem mundane. All the paperwork, meetings, and seminars could kill the ability to believe that we are making a difference, but every time I go back to the Leuser Ecosystem and meet the local communities, rangers, and field teams who stand on the front line of conserving this incredible ecosystem—I feel re-energized and re-inspired to do more on my part to join the fight. I enjoy doing this work because I feel passionate about doing things for places I love. The "boring" work of sitting in a meeting or being in court-room becomes more meaningful when one understands how it fits in the bigger picture.

The bigger picture of conservation in the Leuser Ecosystem means com-batting ecologically devastating activities such as expansion of palm oil plantations, mining, logging, new settlements, and new roads. It means not sitting still and watching the profits obtained from forest destruction go to a few corporations or political elites, instead of funneling back into the community. It means dealing with one of the highest deforestation rates in the world. "The part that make me really angry," says Farwiza, "is the realization that dying nature (in the Leuser Ecosystem) is not a process that's happening naturally. It's a process driven by greed and desire to consume beyond what the planet can sustain. Yet, as one of my mentors once said, 'Be angry—anger fuels resolution.'"

Unfortunately, such an incident of unsustainable greed and environmental destruction first brought international attention to the Leuser Ecosystem and Farwiza's work with HAkA. In 2013, the Indonesian Minister of the Environment sued the palm oil company PT Kallista Alam for illegally burning and destroying the Tripa Peat Swamp in the Leuser Ecosystem. Farwiza was called in as a factual witness, to describe what she had seen happening. While she was glad to be able to testify against the destructive practices of the company, she says, "The court proceeding could be intimidating at times. The lawyers grill and question you and every aspect of your life. They try to twist things around to take away the legitimacy of your word, as if you're biased or dishonest despite being under oath." She wasn't scared, and relished the opportunity to speak, but other witnesses from the local community were terrified and saw the company as a massive force that could make their lives very difficult.

After a hard-fought three-year campaign that included four court cases and eleven court decisions, Indonesia's Supreme Court in Jakarta found the company guilty of deliberately burning the peatlands, and they were forced to pay 30 million US dollars in fines and restorations costs. "This was unprecedented in Indonesia," says Farhan. "It had never happened before. Everyone around the world who signed petitions, participated in days of action, donated their time and money to HAkA, and covered the story helped make it happen." The court decision was a key moment in Farwiza's life, too. "It was through these experiences of being in the courtroom and testifying against the palm oil company when I thought to myself, this is what I was meant to do."

Farwiza's conservation victories haven't just been in the courts; some have happened on a more personal level. "My father used to imagine us getting rich from him either being a logger, a palm oil grower, or aquaculture farm owner," she says. And he encouraged her to go into business to earn a living as well. "Over time, our clash of ideas and interactions has turned him into one of the biggest advocates for the protection of the Leuser Ecosystem. During the time he served in the parliament between 2000 and 2014, he has changed his view about the forest and resources contained within it, and he did what he could to strengthen protection for the Leuser Ecosystem, instead of supporting people to strip it bare and harvest the resources within."

In 2016, in honor of her work with HAkA, Farwiza was awarded a prestigious Whitley Award from the Whitley Fund for Nature (WFN), a British nonprofit that for the past twenty-three years has been offering a financial prize and ongoing support to outstanding nature conservationists around the developing world. Farwiza is using her prize winnings to fight another battle for the Leuser Ecosystem: the 2013 proposed Spatial Plan, recommended by the Aceh government, which she says "fails to recognize Leuser as an important area for conservation and, if approved, would effectively legalize oil palm plantations, logging, mining, and road development inside the protected area. The Spatial Plan will dismantle protection of important habitat, destroy forests, and make way for exploitative industries."

Farwiza is fighting the plan by helping to bring attention to the issue through public and legal means—citizen lawsuits against proposed construction plans—and by working to ensure that community concerns are included in land-use and conservation policies at a government level. Her goal is to shift the balance of power to a local level and empower communities to take direct action to defend *their forest*. "The biggest problem we are facing right now is that we need to fight our own government to protect our own forest, our own land, and our own people," she says. "It's not just a loss of biodiversity and extinction. With four million people living within and around the Leuser Ecosystem, it's a matter of our community's survival. We survived civil conflict. We survived the tsunami. We won't survive the new waves of natural disaster if the forest is destroyed en masse."

To Farwiza, conservation is not a career, but a life choice that she continues to reassess and remake every day. "I allow my passion to drive me forward inch by inch. I am a very persistent conservation enthusiast who would like to see stronger protection over wild places." She does not see the rewards for her work in financial compensation, but in getting to live life on her own terms. "I get to work flexible hours and do pretty much whatever I want, although the number of hours I put in end up exceeding normal working hours, but it never gets boring. I rarely dread Monday. I look forward to getting to work and delivering," she says. "Interaction with nature and wildlife is also a big personal payoff."

Two particular interactions with wildlife stand out for her. The first occurred in 2012 when Farwiza was part of a team that included Dr. Ian Singleton of the Sumatran Orangutan Conservation Program (SOCP), the NGO Yayasan Ecosystem Lestari (foundation for a sustainable ecosystem), the Nature and Natural Resource Conservation Agency of Indonesia (BKSDA), and the police to help rescue an orangutan from the hands of a wildlife trader. She describes what happened:

> The trader brought out this tiny orangutan. Roughly and with no compassion, he dumped it on the floor of this dark room with a tiny bit of light coming from the back door. We (Farwiza and members of the group Wildlife Asia) were posing to be buyers. I asked how old the orangutan was. The man said the baby was two months old and told us that his parents had abandoned him. I picked him up, and he was so small and light and also defensive and angry, trying to bite anything. We told the man we would be back tomorrow with the funds. We contacted Dr. Ian Singleton and he brought his team, the police, and government officials. But when we came back the next day to confiscate the animal, the trader was hiding him. It took days of us working with various local authorities, but we finally found out where the baby was and the trader surrendered him to the police. Ian took him to a rehabilitation center, and they found out that he was not a baby, but a very undernourished three-year-old animal. The great news is that in 2016 the orangutan (who was named Chocolate) was released into the Jantho forest.

A second wildlife interaction she recalls is the time she met Rosa, a baby elephant who had been relocated to the government-run Saree Elephant Rescue Center after her father and several other elephants had been killed. "She was my first contact with a baby elephant and I would visit her often," says Farwiza. "It was new and exciting for me. She was like a puppy. We would play. I had seen so many photos of baby elephants, but until her I had not fallen in love with an elephant. I did not live near her but would visit her as often as I could." Sadly, Rosa died in 2016 of an elephant herpes virus.

Sad stories in Leuser are all too abundant. With such small populations of four iconic species, time is of the essence. Every endangered elephant, rhino, tiger, or orangutan killed brings the population one step closer to extinction, which is one of the reasons Farwiza doesn't give up. "I've made choices and some of these choices might seem like a sacrifice for other people, but not for me," she says. "Some people think I am crazy to have given up the conveniences I have abroad and a relationship with a man who I thought at the time was the love of my life because I simply can't give up Leuser. I chose to stay in Aceh, working to protect Leuser, instead of jumping on a plane to be with him. I've turned down numerous well-paying job offers because they don't align with my passion or something I really care about."

Although Farwiza doesn't give up, won't give up, and in fact it could be said she lives for the Leuser Ecosystem, she has her quiet moments when her work and her efforts feel futile, when quitting occupies a nagging space in the back of her mind. "There are times when, on a personal level, I feel I can't do this anymore. During those periods, the challenge feels ten times bigger, as I simply have no energy to cope with anything. I have a mantra that I repeat to myself when I feel like I can't cope: 'It's hard now, but it will pass'—it might sound cliché but slowly, over time, it works." Nature is another remedy for the bouts of frustration and depression that Farwiza sometimes feels. "I try to spend as much time in nature as possible to remind myself what the energy is that drives me."

With over half of the world population living in densely populated, urban areas, access to wildlife and wild places is something Farwiza believes seems remote and luxurious to many people. "Instead of roaming the jungle or diving the ocean depth for food, we simply go to the grocery store. Instead of getting water from a well, we simply turn the tap," she says. "Convenience has made a lot of us think of nature simply as a holiday destination instead of a crucial life-support system. To remedy this disconnect from nature and the services it provides, Farwiza would like to see a shift from a "development versus conservation" mindset to a more inclusive "conservation for development" mindset. "In my opinion, this connectedness can be created through encouraging more interactions with nature," she says. "From child-like curiosity about trees and insects to a growing understanding about ecosystem functions, if we allow ourselves to be educated about the natural world, it's hard not to fall in love with it."

Farwiza is also philosophical in contemplating the role each person can play in conservation. "Every little bit counts," she says. "Most people might not pick up a gun or hunt wildlife or purchase ivory or rhino horn, but by purchasing products from commodities that destroy the habitat of these endangered species, we unintentionally contribute to the demise of these species. It's the sum of all the small things we all do that matters. By being smart consumers, anyone can become an advocate of the Leuser Ecosystem."

When Farwiza won the Whitley Award, Sir David Attenborough, narrator of BBCs *Blue Planet*, one of Farwiza's heroes, and a trustee of the Whitley Fund for Nature, said: "Whitley Award winners are simply exceptional people—passionate individuals who are committed to achieving positive environmental impact and long-term conservation and community benefits."

Farwiza Farhan embodies every word of that description.

For more information on Farwiza Farhan, please visit www.haka.or.id.

CHAPTER 17

• • •

Dominique Bikaba:
Gorilla Warrior

"This forest is everything to me. I'd say my life is based on this forest."

—Dominique Bikaba

Credit: Daniel Fox/Jackson Hole Wildlife Film Festival & Conservation Summit

Dominique Bikaba.

IN 2004, WHEN REBEL FORCES surrounded the home of Dominique Bikaba in the Democratic Republic of Congo (DRC), he jumped out of a window and tumbled into the garden. At around 4 a.m., after hours of lying on the ground in complete silence, he heard an explosion. The rebels had blown up the town's central electrical lines, casting his village in complete darkness. Using the dark as a cover, Bikaba slipped away to safety, where people in the community hid him. When he returned home a week later, he found everything in his house had been destroyed or looted. Later, after repeated attacks, he was forced to leave his village and relocate to another town for his protection.

The DRC, a land rich in natural resources and beauty, has suffered some of the worst violence in African history. In the past thirty years, a deadly blend of dictators, militias, and warlords has claimed upwards of five million human lives. The wars and fighting have wreaked havoc not just on people, but also on the land and the wildlife of the Congo basin forest, the second largest rainforest in the world, which is home to numerous endemic and protected species, including the eastern lowland gorilla.

Rather than hiding from danger, Bikaba has sacrificed his safety, risking armed robbery, rebel attacks, and kidnapping in order to protect the gorillas, the forest, and the land of the eastern Congo that is his home.

🐾

Bikaba was born in 1972 in Chombo, a small village in eastern DRC that borders Rwanda. The land of his birth, a biologically diverse ecosystem within the Congo basin forest, is home to critically endangered eastern lowland gorillas, chimpanzees, forest elephants, and many other rare species. In 1970, the government, under the dictator Mobutu Sésé Seko, decided to establish an area of about 2,300 square miles as Kahuzi-Biega National Park (KBNP)—an area that was expanded to ten times its original size in 1975. Although in 1937 European colonialists had designated the area as the Kahuzi Zoological and Forest Reserve, the designation as a national park meant the forced evacuation of local and indigenous communities who lived inside the new boundaries on their traditional lands. Many of those expulsed were indigenous Pygmies, forest dwellers who live by subsistence hunting and gathering. "Nobody knows how many people exactly were forced to leave at that time," says Bikaba.

Bikaba's family was also expelled from their traditional land with no governmental plan as to where they would go or how they would make a living. Bikaba was then taken from his parents and sent to live with his grandmother, who lived outside of the forest. It was with his grandmother that Bikaba came to love wildlife and wild places. "My grandmother took me into the forest with her for many hours each day," explains Bikaba. "While in the forest she taught me about the plants and animals."

Bikaba also learned about wildlife through direct experience with some of the DRC's most charismatic animals. "I was just a small child, so when wildlife came into my grandmother's fields to feed on crops, I would be on her back when she chased them away with just her hands or a stick," he says. His grandmother tangled with male baboons that came to feed on her sorghum and pumpkins. She had encounters with gorillas and, at times, with elephants. One elephant encounter in particular stands out for Bikaba.

When he was about thirteen, a bull elephant came to raid his grandmother's crops. Bikaba, a stick in his hand, and his grandmother with a machete in hers, walked up behind the animal. When the bull was about twenty feet from where the two stood, he looked at them, then turned and headed back towards the forest. "Elephants are very big and powerful and can kill many people," explains Bikaba. "But when it saw my grandmother, it just left, like it knew it was on someone else's area."

The indigenous Pygmy people living in the village of Buyungule, about one mile from the park, also helped to raise Bikaba and inspire his love of the forest and its inhabitants. "At the time of my childhood, a Pygmy woman named M'Bidiku, the Pygmy chief's wife, had a son of the same age as me," says Bikaba. "She took me and nursed me along with her own son." Although the Pygmy tribe had been expelled from their land and were suffering great hardship, they found the heart and the love to care for Bikaba. "They took me into their huts, feeding me with their food and letting me sleep while my grandmother was in the fields. When my grandmother would come back in the evening, my Pygmy mom would take me back to her." Today, Bikaba considers his grandmother (who passed away in 2002) and his Pygmy mother the most important influences on his life. "Genetically I am not a Pygmy," he says, "but, I am one because they raised me."

Once in high school, Bikaba received an A-level diploma in biochemistry. With such strong grades and a mind for science, he dreamed of studying nuclear chemistry in college, but his family did not have the money to send him to Kinshasa, the capital city, to pursue his studies. Meanwhile, he was concerned by what was happening with the Pygmies. After they lost their traditional land and their access to the forest and means for subsistence, they started stealing other farmers' crops to survive. "They were often injured or killed when caught stealing on other farmer's lands," explains Bikaba. Teaching the Pygmy people to farm and helping them to find alternative livelihoods, he knew, was not a matter of choice. It was a matter of survival. As such, he has worked hard to get permanent lands restored to them. Even when he has not been as successful in this goal as he would've liked, he says, "I have no regrets in actions I have taken for my causes even if some didn't work out the way I planned them. I just learned from my failures."

At the same time he was concerned about the people, he was concerned about the wildlife, the eastern lowland gorilla—the largest living primate—in particular. Bikaba wanted a job within the park to help mitigate human-wildlife conflict, but getting this type of work was competitive, and he was young, so instead of going to work for the park, in 1992, he and John Kahekwa, Gervais Igugu, and David Bismwa co-founded the first local conservation organization in his region called the Pole Pole Foundation (POPOF). The goal of POPOF was to help resolve conflict between the parks and the surrounding communities. With his goal in mind, Bikaba led POPOF to implement reforestation projects around KBNP. He also started educational outreach and public awareness to involve local and indigenous communities in the long-term preservation of the park and of their community.

In 1993, while still working for POPOF, Bikaba decided to go to college. He attended the Higher Institute of Rural Development of Bukavu, where he specialized in regional planning. He did the first three years of course work and then, as required by the college, set out to gain more professional experience before he could come back and finish his degree.

Bikaba's completion of his first three years in 1996 also marked the beginning of turbulent times in the DRC. The 1994 genocide in Rwanda had created hundreds of thousands of refugees, many of whom streamed into the eastern DRC, often living less than a mile from the park. "With no resources, money, or security, the refugees were forced to cut down trees," he says. By 1998, POPOF had planted approximately twenty-one thousand trees, but Bikaba explains, "With so many people and no management plan, the refugees devastated our tree plantations."

The refugee crisis formed the backdrop for another devastating situation: the First Congolese War (1996–97), which ousted Mobutu

Sésé Seko, who had been military dictator and president of Zaire (now DRC) since 1965. The invasion of Zaire in 1996 that replaced Mobutu with rebel leader Laurent Kabila brought little change from the corrupt policies of his predecessor, and a second Congo War that lasted until 2003 followed. These wars impacted the DRC socially, economically, and environmentally, creating severe human rights abuses and taking a toll on the land and its wildlife.

Before the wars, there were approximately seventeen thousand eastern lowland gorillas. In 2016, the population was thought to be as low as 3,800 (due to violence in the region, the exact population is unknown), with the majority of them living in KBNP. "The foreign troops and rebels didn't care about our gorillas," says Bikaba. "Between 1998 and 2004, half of the 263 gorillas were slaughtered in the original highland part of the park."

One crushing event in particular from this time has stayed with Bikaba. "In 1997, when my area and the park were under control of foreign armed troops, the troops shot Ninja, a famous silverback gorilla, and brought his body to the park station, which was transformed into a military outpost at that time," he says. "Seeing his dead body with a sign of a bullet in the head was a horrible shock." Although Bikaba cared about all the gorillas, Ninja had been close to his heart. "We had been making postcards of him and we were selling them to fundraise for our projects." The rebel violence surrounding the murder of Ninja got worse, the kind of terror that a person never forgets. "It is a taboo in my culture to eat gorilla flesh," explains Bikaba. "But those Rwandan soldiers knew our culture and how breaking a taboo would affect people, so they forced every person who passed by to eat Ninja's meat. Whoever refused was shot dead directly. It is hard to forget when some of the people who were killed are from your area."

With this sort of violence destabilizing the country and with his continued work in eastern DRC, Bikaba himself has often been in danger. "Rwandan-backed rebels living in and around KBNP wanted to extend their power and control over communities," he says. They knew Bikaba's work influenced many people, including important community leaders. "They don't see conservation," he says, "they see the power you have over the communities and how you could drive them against the rebels." If the rebels suspected that he did not support their missions, he became a target of their violence. "Because I worked in the forest and

I knew where they were hiding and sometimes knew strategic information, they targeted me," he says. The attack against Bikaba in 2004, carried out by the Rwandan-backed National Congress for the Defense of People (CNDP), was one such incident of violence. In 2010, Bikaba was the victim of targeted armed robbery, and in 2015, his computer and all of his backup devices were stolen.

It isn't just Bikaba who has been targeted. In 2009, his mother and five other people in his village were shot. Bikaba's mother was the only one who survived. "My mother spent five months in hospital," he says. "She received two bullets in her thigh and one in her hand. Maybe they targeted her because she was my mom," he says, although he is not sure if this is the case, nor is he sure who was behind the killings.

It's especially difficult to pinpoint perpetrators, as the violence isn't just from rebels. It's from displaced peoples as well. "The most difficult part of my work, besides the political unrest and violence, is dealing with people who are impoverished, asking them to leave their traditional subsistence activities without always being able to provide sustainable alternatives," he says. "Whatever good they might feel for conservation, it's difficult to maintain these programs if the people don't have alternative livelihoods and you can't get buy-in. After three generations, some people still believe that their traditional lands are in the park. Other people don't have an option and they live on poaching activities in the park. Some of these people are armed."

Despite the violence, Bikaba continued his work with POPOF, and in 2004 he received a scholarship from the "Education First Program" through Partners in Conservation (PIC) at the Columbus Zoo to finish his degree in regional planning at the same college (Higher Institute of Rural Development of Bukavu). In 2009, due to internal issues in POPOF, he left the organization and started Strong Roots Congo, which he remains in charge of today.

The mission of Strong Roots Congo is the involvement of local and indigenous communities in the long-term preservation of protected areas in the DRC. Because Bikaba knows that peace between the people and peace with the environment are interconnected, he says, "As a conservationist, I am not only focused on the forest and on wildlife, but on communities." Bikaba wants conservation to advance from its outdated, colonial origins that took away land from locals and excluded them from decision making, to a concept that empowers local communities and includes them in decision making. "My work has taught me to have a big heart, not necessarily a big brain. Sometimes you don't need high-tech software, you need just to be a human."

With its focus on research, conservation, and sustainable development through education and the empowerment of local and indigenous communities, Strong Roots has accomplished many projects, including artisan cooperatives, environmental education, health and conservation, primate protection, Pygmy land projects, retraining of miners, and reforestation. Regarding restoration, Bikaba says, "I want to bring the forest to the villagers by giving them saplings to grow on their own farms, providing trees to communities so they don't cut them down in the park." As of 2016, Strong Roots had given out and planted about two million trees around the park—trees that have become firewood, houses, and school desks and that would otherwise be felled from inside the park.

Outside of deforestation, one of the biggest conservation threats in the DRC is illegal mining, often associated with militias and armed conflict. The incredible mineral wealth of the DRC contains numerous elements and includes cobalt, coltan, copper, cadmium, iron ore, tin, tungsten, diamonds, gold, silver, and zinc. These minerals are often used as blood, or conflict, minerals—minerals whose price tag helps fund violence, human rights abuses, and environmental degradation.

Most mines in eastern Congo, according to Bikaba, have some connection to militias, whether it is through direct control or through the demanding of "taxes" from workers to militias. Various militias have been fighting each other in east Congo for more than a decade, relying on illegal mining to fund their activities. And it isn't just humans that illegal mining affects, it's gorillas. From the toll of deforestation and habitat loss associated with the mines to creating greater access for migrants who hunt gorillas for bush meat and the illegal wildlife trade, the animals suffer. "The palm oil threat for orangutans in Indonesia is what minerals are for gorillas in DRC."

In 2010, Bikaba testified before the United States Congress in support of the Dodd-Frank Act. Although largely a financial reform law, section 1502 of Dodd-Frank included legislation about conflict minerals in the DRC. At the time Bikaba testified, conflict minerals were generating an estimated $183 million each year for armed groups in eastern DRC.

President Obama passed Dodd-Frank on July 21, 2010, requiring manufactures to conduct "conflict-free" audits and carefully trace their supply chain. While the provision doesn't ban companies from importing conflict minerals into the United States, companies have to publish the information on their websites, allowing consumers to choose which products to purchase. Although conflict gold remains an issue in the DRC, Dodd-Frank significantly reduced the involvement of armed groups in the "3T" minerals—tin, tantalum, and tungsten—minerals that are essential in the manufacture of many electronic devices, including mobile phones and laptops.

Bikaba is thrilled that the law passed in the United States. "It helped a lot, keeping pressure on security processes in eastern DRC and in drafting mineral certification, which today provides socioeconomic assets for artisanal miners (small-scale subsistence miners) and supports livelihoods for rural communities." Bikaba further helps combat illegal mining with programs at Strong Roots that work with miners and former miners to help form mining co-ops and to provide other alternatives to mining in protected areas. The cessation of illegal mining also has significant consequences for wildlife, as illegal mining has been the biggest cause of gorilla decline in the last twenty years. "If illegal mining is stopped in protected areas," says Bikaba, "then gorillas will survive."

Outside of his work with Strong Roots, Bikaba has been conducting long-term academic research on gorillas and chimpanzees in KBNP since 1995. He coauthored an important paper on great primates: *Long-Term Research on Grauer's Gorillas in Kahuzi-Biega National Park, DRC, Life History, Foraging Strategies, and Ecological Differentiation from Sympatric Chimpanzees* (2012). The research from this paper provided insight into the reproductive conservation strategies for gorillas and chimpanzees that occupied the same or overlapping geographic areas. One of their findings was that infanticide by male gorillas had not been reported in KBNP until after the large-scale killing of their populations in the 1990s, when its occurrence became frequent.

As Bibaka learned more about these endangered animals, he realized he wanted to get deeper into research. In order to do so, he felt he needed more academic training. He was thinking about enrolling at Oxford for a master's degree in biodiversity, conservation, and management, but on a trip to Japan in 2010 to give a talk on primate conservation, he met artist Ann Oberkirch, who had just returned from trekking in Uganda and Rwanda to see gorillas. The two exchanged information and Oberkirch told Bikaba about the School of Forestry and Environmental Studies at Yale, which was close to her home in the United States. She gathered all the information for Bikaba and encouraged him to apply.

Bikaba thought it sounded like a good match, and he started the arduous application process. Because English was not his first language, he had to take English placement tests along with the required GRE entrance exams. After a hectic year in which test results got lost and Yale couldn't process his application, he was admitted. In 2013 he finally left the DRC for the Yale School of Forestry and Environmental Studies. "Yale was a wonderful community. It was a family," he says. "I was taken by the university's process and rigor and by the faculty members and students and the whole community that assisted every single moment that I needed it."

One month before graduating from Yale, the European branch of Development Alternatives, Inc., an NGO that works to "tackle fundamental social and economic development problems caused by inefficient markets, ineffective governance, and instability," hired him to monitor and evaluate a DFID (UK Department for International Development) road construction program in eastern DRC. "The program focused on how constructing strategic roads could contribute to stabilization of security, communities, and socioeconomic development," he explains. "It also monitored the impact the roads would have on natural resources exploitation." Although the job was mired in politics, he was passionate about the work, which allowed him to combine research with conservation and development.

After eighteen months at this job, he was hired by the Wildlife Conservation Society (WCS) to lead a USAID-funded conservation program in the biologically diverse, complex, and important Maiko-Tayna-Kahuzi-Biega and Itombwe landscape (MTKB), covering the ranges of both the eastern lowland gorilla and the eastern chimpanzee. He also continued to contribute to the work of Strong Roots when needed. "I am now working on a gorilla habitat connectivity project, which spans protected areas and unprotected forests where they live," he says. "I believe that if relict gorilla populations are connected, they may have a chance to increase in numbers again and hopefully to reverse their critical decline, which appeared these last two decades. The most rewarding part of my work is contributing to the protection and survival of a unique and endemic gorilla subspecies, along with other taxa and their habitat, and contributing to sustaining pride in my country."

For Bikaba, the personal payoffs are not monetary. "The personal payoffs are the respect I have from my community, the numerous others who now engage in conservation to preserve relict rainforest and traditional lands for future generations. I have trained young people who will continue this work after me. Many of the community members didn't know that they could contribute to the park's preservation. They considered the park as belonging to white people or to the Congolese Wildlife Authority." That attitude is starting to change. Kids in villages now want to "be like Dominique."

Having trained young people to follow in his footsteps and work toward conservation, he believes education is a key tool to inspire the next generation to care about wildlife and wild places. He wants everyone to integrate conservation into his or her thinking. "If you only have a minute, think about how humans and wildlife are linked," he says. "If you have a day, share with friends and families about your experience with wildlife and ask them to engage for wildlife conservation. If you have a year, contribute in any way to preserve a species somewhere. This can be a financial contribution, even with one dollar, or it can be by running a wildlife conservation campaign or attending a wildlife conservation conference. If you have a lifetime, visit wildlife somewhere in its natural habitat. Do not expect results in one week," he advises. "Set long-term goals. Conservation is the work of a lifetime."

Bikaba has had such a lifetime so far with both gorillas and guerillas. He understands that in war zones, sustainable peace is a requirement for achieving lasting conservation. And he will keep fighting on behalf of the land, the people, and the wildlife of the DRC.

For more information on Dominque Bikaba, please visit www.strongrootscongo.org.

CHAPTER 18

• • •

Craig Packer, PhD:
Outspoken Champion
of Africa's Lions

*"We have to accept global responsibility for global
treasures like the Serengeti."*

—Dr. Craig Packer

Credit: Robert Caputo

Craig Packer.

TWO BILLION DOLLARS A YEAR would do it. That's the number
Craig Packer, largely considered the world's leading expert on lions, thinks the global community needs to contribute to protect Africa's
wildlife. This number is no off-the-cuff figure. It's taken Packer nearly
four decades of studying lions to arrive at the amount. Smaller projects

are great, but to really make a difference, to protect what he calls "world heritage species" for the next century, the price tag is big. And it's one the entire world must shoulder.

After nearly half a century of working in Tanzania (until he lost his research permit in 2013 for his stand against trophy hunting), Packer has come up with what he calls "realpolitik" conservation solutions for protecting animals the world values. Packer's "realpolitik" approach might not always make him popular, but popularity isn't his goal; answering scientific questions and solving problems is.

🐾

As a child growing up in Fort Worth, Texas, Packer loved nature and the outdoors. He had an insatiable curiosity for exploring the universe in whatever form, whether it be large or small, and moreover, he loved being outside. Due to family circumstances, he spent a lot of time away from the city and on his grandmother's farm in the small town of Noodle, about thirty miles outside Fort Worth, a place, he jokes, that actually exists, despite its curious name. "Spending my summers on the farm I was always outdoors. I liked to go hunting and fishing. I always hoped when I grew up I could find something to do that would allow me to be outdoors." When he reached junior high, his scientific curiosity deepened and he wanted to explore the bigger questions of evolution. "I thought evolution was the most amazing thing. Look out the window and you're looking at the consequences of hundreds of millions of years." Intellectually stimulated and eager to learn, he set out to do a science fair project on the topic. Unfortunately, his biology teacher, influenced by Christian fundamentalism, wouldn't permit him to go forward with his scientific ideas. In order to pursue them, he would have to wait to study evolution until college.

In 1971, Packer started college at Stanford studying engineering, but he soon decided that was too boring for him and turned to human biology. When Packer was twenty-one, Paul Ehrlich, the renowned ecologist and author of *The Population Bomb* (1968), came to speak to his ecology class. "He had just come back from Africa and showed pictures of zebra," recalls Packer. "I thought they were so cool and I thought it would be great to go and see them." When Ehrlich told the class that primatologist Dr. Jane Goodall had a new program, which allowed students to go to Gombe Stream National Park in Tanzania and work as field assistants, Packer was instantly intrigued. "I didn't know who Jane Goodall was. I had no special interest in primates, but I wanted to see zebras. I applied and it was over." He was accepted and set off for Gombe, where he met not just Jane Goodall, but also the species that would become his first study subject: baboons. Although Packer's most influential work has been with lions, he got his start in evolutionary biology with primates.

Packer quickly grew fascinated with the soap opera-like drama within a baboon troop. "I'd always been interested in evolution and I was so fascinated to think that these animals behaved in ways that reflected the real challenges of life—finding a mate, finding food—and they had their own unique solutions in a way that fit their environment."

Perhaps on some level Packer could relate to the animals he studied, as he, too, faced many of the same predicaments as those of a juvenile male baboon. Packer was twenty-one at the time, on his own, far from home, about to graduate college, and unsure as to what he'd do next. Similarly, a juvenile male baboon was on his own, looking to leave home—although in this case for a female to mate with—and facing myriad dangers, such as full-grown males trying to prevent young competitors from joining their troop and mating with "their" females. "What captured my imagination was watching adolescent baboons and how they had to move. They had to go to a different troop. They'd do it by themselves and it was scary for them, but they had this inner drive." (Their inner drive was to find a female, and it just so happens that although ultimately finding a mate was not his driving force, Packer did meet his first wife while in Gombe.)

With his interest in baboons sparked, Packer decided to stay in Gombe. He thought he'd "rather chase monkeys" than head off to medical school at the University of Texas in Houston, where he'd been accepted. Because many of Goodall's previous field assistants had recently left, she asked Packer to assist with her long-term study of baboons. "One day we were on the beach at Lake Tanganyika watching baboons. A young female named Clover had been eating sticky fruit from a tree," says Packer. "There was this sticky latex-like substance on her lips. She picked up a corncob and wiped her mouth with it. Jane said, 'that's tool use.'" Goodall had witnessed tool use in chimpanzees, but this was the first time it had been documented in baboons. Packer snapped a photo.

When the photo and the article came out in the prestigious scientific journal *Nature,* in 1973, Packer thought, maybe I can do this for a career.

He left Gombe in 1972 and headed to the University of Sussex for his PhD. In those days there were no programs on animal behavior in the United States. Yet, as the Nobel Prize for Physiology was awarded to Konrad Lorenz (Austria), Nikolaas Tinbergen (the Netherlands), and Karl von Frisch (Austria) in 1973 for their work on social behavior in animals, the field was burgeoning in Europe. After he finished his dissertation, Packer once again, like the baboons he studied, had to figure out what to do next. He and his wife at the time set out to Japan to study Japanese macaques, but, as Packer explains, "It turns out the Japanese were too polite to tell us there was no space left for new researchers to work on the project." They had to look for alternatives. In 1978, friends who worked on the Serengeti Lion Project in Tanzania, a project that was already more than a decade old, needed someone to take over the research. Packer decided to give it a try.

Three years after he'd left Africa, he was back.

🐾

Lions are boring study subjects.

At least that's what Packer initially thought. "When you look into a baboon's eyes, you can see the gears turning in there. When you look into a lion's eyes, it's cold fish. It's not the same. So I didn't get that connection with lions. Plus, lions sleep all the time." In fact, lions can sleep for roughly twenty hours a day.

Packer was frustrated at the lack of action from the lions. "You never see them do anything and mostly what they do is in the dark. We might see something interesting and active like every two weeks." But on the other hand, he found lions to be interesting intellectually. Whereas most cats are solitary, lions do everything in groups—groups of females, groups of males, mixed groups. Packer wanted to understand not just lion behavior, but how their behaviors had evolved, so he decided to stay with the lion project. At the end of three years, he was a lion convert. Studying lions, he realized, was amazing. In 1983, he took a faculty position at the University of Minnesota as professor of ecology, evolution, and behavior, a position he still holds in 2016. Working at the university allowed him to divide his time between the United States and Africa, and to expand the scope of his studies, as he now had graduate students to help him with his research.

With the decades of research Packer and his myriad of graduate students have given to lions, he has become a leading expert on their ecology. Besides his work on canine distemper virus (a viral disease that affects a wide variety of animal families and in an outbreak case in 1994 was spread to lions from domestic dogs), some of the questions he has answered are: Why do lions live in groups? How does the moon affect human-lion conflict? Is it better to be a dark-maned or a light-maned lion?

On why lions live in groups, Packer says it's not for hunting purposes, as many *National Geographic* documentaries lead people to believe. It's about territory. "In the savanna there are well identified 'high value' geographic locations that can best be defended by groups," says Packer. "It helps to be obnoxious in a group. Lion gang warfare," he says, "dominates the savanna."

In terms of the moon, Packer found out that a full moon makes for a bright night when an ambush predator, such as the lion, has less of a chance of being successful and therefore is less likely to hunt. When the moon is below the horizon and the night sky is dark, lions have the advantage—and this is when man-eating lions catch most of their victims. Packer recounts the saying of the Bushmen: "When the moon is up, it's human time. When moon is down, that's lion time."

As for the dark mane versus light mane question, his research team has been able to employ an approach that would make most children jealous: four life-sized, stuffed lions. Placing different-color maned lions—named Lothario, Romeo, Fabio, and Julio (as in Iglesias)—in the range of a female in heat and then in the presence of another male, Packer and his students found out that darker manes attract females and intimidate males. Darker manes, it turns out, are an indicator of the overall fitness of a lion: A lion has to be in great physical shape to support a dark mane.

Science makes Packer happy; tangling with the Tanzanian government, not so much. And it was the question of manes that led to the entanglement.

Starting in 1999, trophy hunters started coming to Packer and his team, telling them that there were maneless males living outside the Serengeti. Packer didn't believe it. These hunters kept insisting, so Packer investigated. It turns out that the hunters were right. There were maneless males, not because they were some new species, but because they were adolescents, lions not yet old enough to grow a mane. With typical scientific precision, Packer and students set out to quantify the effect hunting young male lions had on the lion population.

What Packer learned had to do with lions' complex social system. A male lion will breed at about age four and then stay with his cubs to protect them from other males for two years—until the cub is self-sufficient enough to defend itself. However, if this breeding male is killed and another male lion comes in, the new lion will kill the cubs in order to replace them with his own. This practice, known as infanticide, essentially means that every time a father lion is killed, so are the cubs, thus accelerating the decline in the population. To Packer, there was a logical, scientific solution: Don't kill male lions under the age of six. If this recommendation is practiced, he believes trophy hunting, though not something he is morally fond of, is sustainable. He even cowrote *A Hunter's Guide to Aging Lions in Eastern and Southern Africa* (2007) to help hunters know how to estimate the age of a lion.

His work led to minimum age requirements for hunting lions in Botswana, Mozambique, Zambia, Zimbabwe, and Tanzania. This was where his troubles with the Tanzanian government escalated. "The reason they were shooting all the young lions in the first place," says Packer, "is because they had shot the old ones. The government was encouraging excessive lion hunting, taking away hunting blocks from operators if they did not shoot enough lions." After Packer's research was published, the Tanzanian government said they would set minimum age requirements, but they wouldn't submit to inspections, and nobody knew if hunters were shooting younger males. "I started complaining. I got too noisy, and in 2013 I lost my research clearance," says Packer. "I'm not even allowed to go into the country. They said I was sabotaging the Tanzanian hunting industry."

All of his work on the minimum age requirement leads to the inevitable issue of whether trophy hunting should be banned altogether, a question Packer is often asked, and one that for him is not black and white. Morally, Packer doesn't agree with trophy hunting, but he believes that if the price tag is high enough and if the money goes back into conservation, trophy hunting can help to protect lions. In fact, hunting operations control four times as much land in Africa as in national parks. "Eighty percent of the lions left are in the hands of hunters," Packer told the *Guardian* in an interview in October 2015. "The problem is the price tag isn't high enough to generate income as the sports hunting industry likes to claim." Whereas Cecil the lion, whose killing in 2015 by an American trophy hunter in Zimbabwe made him the international "poster child" of conservation, was shot for fifty thousand US dollars, the true cost of a tag should've been closer to one million dollars.

The reason Packer believes trophy hunting of lions can even be a part of the panacea of conservation is that if practiced in a sustainable way, it is not inherently damaging to lion populations. Lions, as opposed to larger animals like rhinoceros or elephants, have large litters each year. "Their population can rebound," he says. "As long as you can look after the land, as long as you can keep the needs met for a large number of individuals, the population should be able to persist."

Packer thinks that hunting in and of itself is not the problem: mismanagement and corruption is the issue. In countries where the hunting industry is dominated by corruption, hunters are making a bad situation worse. "They are granted exclusive access to land and generate no money for conservation and it is like strip mining." In countries like South Africa and Namibia where hunting is well managed and the money goes into conservation, Packer believes sport hunting can do a good thing. As for Cecil, Packer adopts a more expansive view. "To me, Cecil was just one dot in a cloud of individuals. I go in a different direction than people who get caught up in the emotions of conservation because they are focused on a specific, individual animal. Something is going to go bad for some animals. This doesn't mean the population is doomed. It is when the number of dots being eliminated is too high that the population goes down."

Packer might be against the morality and mismanagement of trophy hunting, but he also doesn't always see eye-to-eye with animal rights groups such as IFAW (International Fund for Animal Welfare) and ASPCA (American Society for the Prevention of Cruelty to Animals) that oppose sport hunting under any circumstances. As such, Packer is controversial in many circles. "Animal rights groups often think there should be no hunting at all," he says. Local people need to see wildlife as an asset and not a threat, and in many places that is not that case. "Local people," says Packer with his characteristic bluntness, "hate lions."

There is the story he tells of a lion attack on a villager that left him with no arms and a story of the grandmother whose grandchild was taken by a lion; these are the stories of hundreds of Tanzanians killed by lions between 1990 and 2004. "There is no place in the Western world where this would be accepted," he says. In fact, it hasn't been. In America, dangerous predators have been killed off. It was only when the country reached a certain level of economic development that they were brought back. Africa, for the most part, especially in an impoverished country such as Tanzania (expected to be the world's fifth most populated country by the turn of the century), has not reached that stage. Nor have they reached the demographic transition when populations are less impoverished and start to have smaller families. They are living in close proximity to dangerous animals that, as Packer likes to say, "will eat you and your little dog, too." In Maasai country, if a lion kills a cow (as they sometimes do since much of their natural prey has been killed off), there is a one-to-one retaliation rate, meaning for every cow killed, one lion is hunted in retaliation. If a lion kills a person, the situation is far worse. There is the immediate consequence of retaliation, but also the long-term psychological effect on local people. This psychology, of course, elevates fear and animosity.

"We have to keep local people safe and lions out of trouble," says Packer. One way to do this—a means that has earned Packer so many adversaries—is the barrier method: in a word, fences. Places where the lion population is doing well, such as South Africa, have fences. "Fenced reserves have populations closer to the carrying capacity for lions," says Packer. According to Packer, where there are fences, lion populations have positive growth rates. Where there aren't fences, the trend is a downward spiral.

Is it ideal to fence the wilderness? No. But perhaps what is ideal isn't what matters. It's what works. "We are beyond the notion of pristine wilderness," says Packer. His views on conservation might not always make him popular, but he is unafraid of speaking his mind, of alienating himself with animal rights groups, hunters, and even other scientists. He feels that sometimes telling the truth means losing allies.

Then there is the issue of funding. The catchphrase in African conservation is that wildlife should pay its own way. "The problem is we are expecting some of the poorest countries on earth to generate the money to protect the animals," says Packer, "and it's not working." Ecotourism is one model that helps to generate revenue, but it is in no way a cure-all. Governments receive pennies on the dollar from tourist fees. Furthermore, fluctuations in the world economy mean ecotourism is neither a steady nor a reliable business. And what about the less desirable places for tourists—those that are less scenic or have more annoying insects? These places have animals, but not tourists. How are they to pay to care for their wildlife?

Packer's mantra is to adopt conservation on a global scale. He challenges the world to ask how we recognize the value of these animals. "Westerners bear no risk. We pop in for a safari or a hunt and we leave. The most important thing we can do is say it's the world's responsibility to help look after these species. It can't be on the shoulders of the people who can least afford to do it themselves." Conservation on a crowded continent is expensive and it is just going to become even more so as the populations continue to grow.

Packer encourages people to put pressure on major funding institutions such as the International Monetary Fund, UNESCO, and the World Bank to fund African conservation, and he wants everyone who can afford to do so to pitch in a nominal fee—a mere one dollar per person.

Is it realistic? Some say it's not. Is it romantic? Not really. Are people ready? Who knows? But Packer believes that if the world at large does not put money into African conservation, the future is bleak for these animals.

Despite all the obstacles of convincing the world to pay for conservation, despite the opposition to his views and the difficulties he has faced in Tanzania, a quote that Packer says resonates with him is from Samuel Beckett: "Ever tried. Ever failed. No matter. Try again. Fail again. Fail better."

Armed with this philosophy, Packer, a father of two, author of several books and more than one hundred scientific papers, professor and director of the Lion Center at the University of Minnesota, and winner of numerous scientific and academic awards, isn't giving up. "If anything," he says about getting kicked out of Tanzania, "it has freed me up to speak my mind." At the start of 2016, Packer began mentoring a whole new set of graduate students who will focus their research in South Africa and neighboring Botswana. "Botswana is the least corrupt country in Africa—a refreshing contrast from Tanzania," he says. "And the Botswanan wildlife authorities are eager to base their policies on factual information—rather than on the wishes of the hunting industry." As for South Africa, Packer says, "If there are going to be lions anywhere else in Africa in another hundred years, those countries will look a lot like South Africa does today: with private land ownership and fenced reserves. With four times as many people on the continent, and—hopefully—a substantial degree of economic development, the countryside will someday look a lot more like Arizona or New Mexico than the land of Karen Blixen (the author of *Out of Africa,* based on her life while living in Kenya) in the 1890s." But even well-managed fenced reserves face serious challenges, as it can be difficult to maintain any kind of ecological equilibrium with a restricted amount of space. "So anything we learn now in South Africa could be helpful for the future of wildlife management across all of Africa in the coming years."

Packer is also beginning to see the tide turn on some of his ideas. "There is growing recognition about what I am saying about having international subsidies cover the management costs of these African national parks. I hope to bend conservation efforts in that direction with whatever time I have left."

Although conservation on such a grand scale is ambitious, with only about twenty thousand African lions left in the world (with many of them in Tanzania and numbers still plummeting), the global community might want to stir themselves to meet the challenge.

For more information on Craig Packer, please visit www.lionresearch.org.

CHAPTER 19

• • •

Dee Boersma, PhD:
Penguins, a Love Story

"Penguins are our ocean sentinels. They help us understand the effects of pollution, overfishing, and climate change on the marine environment."

—Dr. Dee Boersma

Credit: Dee Boersma

Dee Boersma.

DEE BOERSMA WAS SITTING IN her field house in Punta Tombo, Argentina, where for the last thirty-four years she has spent several months each year, when she thought there was a knock on the metal door. She called out a welcome greeting, but nobody responded. She heard the knock again, and this time she opened the door to find Turbo, a Magellanic penguin. "When I opened the door, he walked right in," says Boersma. Turbo, who Boersma has known for about fourteen years, has never had a serious mate and will often flipper pat or do a circle dance when he sees her, behaviors he would normally display to a female penguin. "I still think he wonders why it is I won't come into his nest," she says, and then adds, "if I could lay Turbo an egg, I would!"

After over forty years of fieldwork with Magellanic penguins and Galápagos penguins, Boersma says, "Penguins wind my clock. They're just cute. They walk upright. They're comical. They're sentient little beings. How could you not fall in love with them?"

Boersma did not set out to be the world's leading penguin biologist, an advocate for their wellbeing, or a fighter for their survival. As a young adult, she planned to be an administrator of a university.

🐾

When Boersma was nine years old, growing up in Ann Arbor, Michigan, her mother gave her a butterfly net and showed her a Cecropia silk moth that she had found dead outside the house. "She wanted me to have a hobby. Being from the Midwest, you take these things seriously," says Boersma. And she did. She turned to butterfly collecting with a passion. "It turns out I loved collecting butterflies and moths. Some things were known about their natural history, but not that much. I wanted to know where they went, so I'd catch one, use a stamp pad to ink its wings, and let it go, so I could see if it was the same one that returned."

Boersma couldn't wait to get to high school and study biology, but when she finally got there, the biology class proved to be a disappointment, as her teacher did not even know what a silk moth was. "I'd been waiting all this time to take biology and the teacher wasn't interested in the things I was interested in," she explains. In college she was excited to take an entomology course, but again, she was disillusioned. "The teacher was really into pesticides and how to kill insects that were pests."

Despite her interest in natural history (which she finally got to explore in an ornithology class), Boersma came from a family of educators and business people, and it was expected she would follow in their footsteps. Her mother was a high school teacher, her father ran a travel company, and her maternal grandfather had been the president of several universities. While her mother wanted her to obtain teaching credentials and her father wanted her to join the family business, Boersma thought that, like her grandfather, she'd become the president of a university.

She studied biology at Central Michigan University, was president of the Student Senate, and, after completing her degree, attended graduate school at Ohio State. Thinking she needed a PhD to become an academic administrator, she asked her mentor, Bill Boyd, president of her alma mater, if it mattered what she got her PhD in. He told her it didn't matter, so she pursued what she loved most, zoology. "I figured if I could get my PhD doing something fun and interesting, that would be good," she says. This decision set her on the path to penguins.

In 1970, Boersma became a PhD student at Ohio State under the mentorship of Dr. Paul Colinvaux, a paleoecologist (someone who studies pollen to understand climate and ecosystems of the past). At the young age of twenty-two, Boersma had not yet fallen in love with penguins, but she knew she wanted to go to the Galápagos Islands, where Darwin had come up with his theory of natural selection, and she knew she wanted to study something that was largely unknown. "I knew there were penguins living on the equator," she says. "And that seemed bizarre."

Colinvaux agreed that Boersma would go to the Galápagos, but, in doing so, he took a risk. "It was still a time of discrimination and a lot of professors said to him, and to me, that they'd never let their female graduate student go to the Galápagos," Boersma recalls. Already she was breaking boundaries in her decision to travel to the remote islands on her own. Boersma looks back at her decision to study a species about which there had only ever been two published reports and says, "I was young and naïve. I had to prove I could do it."

When Boersma got to the archipelago six hundred miles off the coast of South America, she quickly learned that her chances of seeing penguins on Santa Cruz Island, where the Charles Darwin Research Station was located, were nearly nil, as the stronghold for penguins was the island of Fernandina on the western part of the archipelago. The station manager asked her a series of increasingly alarming questions before she got his approval to set out to Fernandina. He asked her if she'd ever camped before. ("I had never camped, since my dad's idea of camping was a five-star hotel, but I knew what I was supposed to say, so I said, 'Oh yeah.'") He asked if she'd ever lived for long periods of time isolated and alone. ("Well, not long periods, but I'm not worried.") After making it clear that such an adventure was risky, as she well knew, she got his permission to go off and find her penguins.

Boersma asked a group of geology graduate students who were headed to Fernandina to climb the volcano and sample gases from the vents if she could pay extra for boat time and be dropped off at Punta Espinosa (in the northeastern part of the island) and then picked up at the end of their expedition about ten days later. They agreed and she started her journey. "I was a little bit worried when I got dropped off," she says. "But there was a tourist guide named David Day, who was staying overnight, waiting to be picked up by a fishing boat the following day. I went up to him and asked what I needed to know about living on the island." Day told her about two things: rice rats and sea lions. Rice rats: they were abundant. They'd want to come into her tent for food. If she didn't keep food in her tent, they'd stay outside, and she'd be okay. Sea lions: they were aggressive. They'd want to be dominant. If she stood her ground when she walked by them, they'd leave her alone, and she'd be okay.

That first night on Fernandina, thanks to Day and his rules, Boersma avoided rice rats, stood her ground with sea lions, and although she did not get to see penguins, she did get to hear them—a sound she describes as lonesome, like a braying donkey: *ha-ha-ha-haaaaaaaaaw*. When she did finally see her first Galápagos penguin the following evening, it was love at first sight. She knew she had picked the right species to study, although she didn't realize how hard it would be.

Boersma describes that first visit to the Galápagos, and every visit since, as magical. "It's like living in a zoo. The animals aren't afraid of you. They're curious," she says. "I got to sleep at night alongside sea lions that sometimes slept resting against the sides of the tent. I'd have to sometimes push against them because they'd snore, and if I jiggled them, they'd wake up, quit snoring, and then go back to sleep." And so she could go back to sleep, too, ready for the next day and her penguins.

🐾

When Boersma came to the Galápagos in 1970, nobody knew much about the Galápagos penguin besides the fact it was the sole penguin living on the equator. Because the small birds tuck themselves away in lava tubes and rocky crevices, often escaping the human eye, no one was even sure of how many there were, where they bred, and how they nested. Boersma has become an expert, learning not just about their biology, but also about threats to their survival.

Part of the threat to Galápagos penguins is natural, due to the dynamics of climate and ocean. The cold water in the deep ocean is full of nutrients. When the cold water and the nutrients are brought near to the surface, due to a subsurface oceanic current called the Equatorial Counter Current, or the Cromwell Current Upwelling, the light allows the phytoplankton—the basic food of the ocean ecosystem—to grow. During an El Niño event, however, the upwelling wanes, surface waters warm, and the food supply plummets. El Niño events occur periodically, but when they occur is unpredictable, and as such, Boersma calls the biology of the Galápagos Islands "predictably unpredictable." As a result of this predictable unpredictability, she says, "The Galápagos penguins are the most flexible species of penguin in the world, adapting their breeding biology and behavior to when food is available for them." For example, in an El Niño year they might not breed, or if they breed they may desert their eggs and chicks to search for food to save themselves. Galápagos penguins molt before they breed instead of when most penguins molt, after breeding. In their unpredictable environment, Galápagos penguins take care of themselves before investing in reproduction.

It is much harder for the penguins to adapt to the anthropogenic changes—those brought on by humans. These threats include overfishing; introduced species such as cats, goats, and rats; climate change (which has led to more frequent and severe El Niño events); and pollution—problems that don't just affect the Galápagos penguins, but all seventeen penguin species world-wide.

Although Boersma continues to study the Galápagos penguin to this day—conducting many projects aimed at increasing their breeding and reproductive success—the small population and unpredictable climate grew frustrating, so for a decade she turned her focus to storm petrels living in a very seasonal environment in Alaska, where oil development and transport tankers would likely threaten seabird populations. Once Boersma showed that storm petrels were ingesting petroleum, she realized she missed the penguins, her first love. In 1982, when Boersma got the chance to go to Argentina for the Wildlife Conservation Society to study Magellanic penguins, she took it.

❦

With more than 200 thousand breeding pairs of Magellanic penguins calling it home, Punta Tombo, Argentina has the largest colony of this charismatic species in the world. A desert-like environment on a peninsula approximately one thousand miles south of Buenos Aires, Punta Tombo is known as the coastal paradise for penguins. While scientists and those who love wildlife see the penguins themselves as part of the paradise and part of the value of the place, others see the paradise and value as purely an economic one.

In 1981, a Japanese firm called Hinode Penguin Company asked the Argentinian government for permission to kill penguins and turn their skins into fashionable golfing gloves, protein, and oil. The public protested the proposed slaughter. Angry Argentinians wrote letters; some even marched to the governor's house to make their voices heard. The plan was scrapped, but William Conway, then director of the New York Zoological Society (now the Wildlife Conservation Society) was working in the region and distressed about what might have happened. He called Boersma, asking her to study the colony. She agreed. "I thought I'd come and study them for a few years," she says. "That was over thirty years ago." She has now led the Magellanic Penguin Project at Punta Tombo since 1982. "I didn't think I'd be doing a long-term study of them," she says. But so little was known about these animals, she had to stay and learn everything she could about them.

And she has learned a lot. Boersma and her graduate students from the University of Washington, working closely with landowners in the Province of Chubut, found out that Magellanic penguins live for thirty years. They discovered that these creatures lay two eggs at an interval of four days apart, which then hatch two days apart. They found out the penguins take sixty to over 120 days to rear their young, and that some are faithful to each other and to their nest sites for years. Boersma and her students discovered that Magellanic penguins do not lay eggs until they are at least four years old and most males are five to eight years old before they find a female, as there are many more males than females. Some males, like Turbo, may never find a mate. They learned that the penguins live in burrows or in bushes, that the best nest sites are those with the best cover from the elements, and that Magellanic penguins can dive close to one hundred yards, hold their breath for 4.6 minutes, and swim more than one hundred miles in twenty-four hours. Over the years they have documented the impacts of climate change, toxic algae blooms, and petroleum on the penguin population.

A typical field day at Punta Tombo means getting up by dawn. The field crew and Boersma head down to the colony before 8 a.m. each day and check nests to see what's happening—which penguins are out and which have stayed behind. She and her students weigh chicks and put satellite tags on penguins so they can track their movements at sea. It was by banding penguins that Boersma knew her friend, Turbo, the door-knocker, was the same friendly bird who had been living under her truck and visiting her all those years. In a 2009 article in the *New York Times*, Boersma called herself "a census taker of the 200,000 breeding pairs of penguins at Punta Tombo." She might also be called the social coordinator of the colony, as she keeps track of who's doing what, who's going where, who's mating with whom, where they're going for their meals, how many chicks they have, and how healthy they are.

In her years of studying and social coordinating, Boersma has discovered a number of disturbing trends. The first of these trends was oil. Between 1982 and 1990, Boersma and her students estimated that about forty-two thousand penguins a year were getting covered in oil and dying. Lax enforcement of laws meant oil tankers going up and down the coast were able to dump their ballast—material that is used to provide stability to the ship, in this case, oily seawater with petroleum—directly into the ocean, so they could cut their costs. Boersma and her team found out that the penguins' preferred migratory routes (moving north in winter to follow the fish and returning south in the spring to breed) overlapped with areas of heavy oil-tanker traffic. The penguins were swimming right through the oily water.

Boersma and her Argentine students went to the Argentinian government to tell them what was happening, but officials didn't want to believe petroleum was killing penguins. Fortunately, Boersma and her students had eight years of data to prove it. Finally, in 1997, the government moved the tanker lanes twenty-five miles offshore. "The effects were dramatic," she says. The number of oiled penguins along the Chubut coastline has since dropped from an estimated forty-two thousand annually to fewer than one hundred. By 2010, no oiled penguins were seen at Punta Tombo.

In 2016, oiled penguins were rare; those that did have oil were returning from their faraway wintering grounds in waters off of Brazil, Uruguay, and even northern Argentina, where laws against oil dumping are less enforced. To add to the already great distance penguins have to travel for food to feed their young, climate change is forcing them to look farther—up to forty miles more than they did a decade ago. The extra foraging distance is a serious problem because while one bird is out searching for food, the other is sitting on the nest, incubating eggs, fasting—all the while losing weight and waiting for their mate to return. "Since the mate has had to swim farther, both parents have to pay the increased cost of travel if they are going to successfully rear their young," says Boersma.

Another concern with climate change is the sheer fact of the heat. Penguins don't have sweat glands. They pant like dogs and dilate their blood vessels to give off heat through their feet and flippers. When they get too hot and are full, blood must be used for digestion and not for cooling, so they overheat. Further, there is the problem of more frequent storms. Boersma has found that increased frequency of storms over the last thirty years has taken a toll on penguins, especially on the chicks. "Punta Tumbo is a desert region. Rain fills up their nests and it's like living in a swimming pool," she explains. "Young penguins are also vulnerable to storms because they don't yet have waterproof feathers. Once they're about five to twenty days old, they're too big to shelter under their parents, so when it rains their down can get wet and they can get cold and die from hypothermia."

Boersma has seen the price penguins are paying for overfishing and the expansion of commercial fisheries. "We're fishing down the food chain," she says in an act of what she calls "vacuuming the seas." Because penguins will eat anything smaller than their heads, expanding fisheries, which take out anything that's edible, compete with penguins for the smallest of the prey. In the Antarctic Peninsula, for example, in the years 2013–14, 210,000 metric tons of krill were removed. In the waters around Peru, four million metric tons per year of anchovy—penguins' favorite food—is harvested annually. It took until 2016 for the province to declare a small marine reserve at Punta Tombo even though 40 percent of the chicks were dying from starvation.

Most of the small fish species being caught are not used to feed humans. They are rendered into fishmeal to feed farm-raised salmon, chickens, and pigs, or made into omega-3 pills. "If you're going to eat an anchovy, eat the whole thing," Boersma says. "Don't eat it indirectly as fishmeal or farm-raised salmon. Turning anchovy into fishmeal is a loss for the environment." Besides not inadvertently consuming anchovy as fishmeal, she advises people to eat sustainable seafood.

While she'd like people to be mindful of what they eat, Boersma acknowledges that being a smart consumer can become a full-time job. Even then, we don't always know the true cost of what we eat. To address this problem, she advocates for a "true-cost administration." Like the Food and Drug Administration helps consumers know the side effects of the drugs they take, she'd like to see a governmental agency that lets consumers know the true cost of the foods or products they buy. "With a conscious economy, we'd all do better," she says. "We're moving in the right direction with fair trade and sustainable seafood, but it still takes a lot of knowledge from the consumer to know the true cost of what they are buying. Penguins are paying our bills, and people should know that. Somebody has to give these creatures a voice. They don't have ballots they can cast. We're in control of their destiny."

Tourism is another concern Boersma has for penguins. While ecotourism can be part of the panacea of conservation, it can also have its drawbacks. For example, in Punta Tombo, increased tourism has led to a higher demand for scarce water resources, more facilities being built in the fragile environment, and sewage being leaked into the sea. "Governments need to manage water, garbage, and the land sustainably and secure a future for penguins," she says.

In 2009, Boersma acted out against a proposed expansion of the tourist trail at Punta Tombo, a boardwalk that would destroy two hundred nests. "This shouldn't be Disneyland," she says. "Tourism is catering to people, but the place should be for penguins too." She calls the kind of tourism—without a guide where people can zip in and out—"bargain-basement tourism" and worries that, like in many places around the world where ecotourism is not well managed, you end up destroying the thing you love. Boersma believes that acting out against the boardwalk trail is a reason the local government did not sign off on her research permit in 2011. "The young director of tourism told me we were just playing with penguins," she says. "The political hassles are the killers."

Despite the drawbacks, Boersma applauds the upsides to tourism. Tourism creates jobs, and then there is the benefit of trained guides who can teach people about what penguins need. Penguins make money, and Boersma would like to see most of that money being used to benefit conservation and the penguins themselves, not getting funneled into general government funds. "Money from penguins should go to help penguins and other wildlife," she says.

Boersma has also tapped into the positive potential of tourism, asking tourists who go to the Galápagos Islands (about 200,000 people each year) to become citizen-scientists and help in her research by sharing their penguin photos with her on www.igalapagos.org. Since 2010, Boersma and her colleagues have raised funds to visit the Galápagos twice a year to check the constructed lava nests they built for penguins. In addition to her visits, she relies on the photographic data collected by thousands of willing eco-tourists. "The Galápagos penguin's reproductive cycle is based on weather conditions, making it difficult to predict when they'll breed successfully, so this is where tourists come in. We rely on photographs from visitors of juvenile or molting penguins to learn what is happening," she says. "By sharing the pictures you take during your travels, you can help us evaluate the health of the penguin population. To know how they're doing we need guides and visitors to be our eyes and help us."

🐾

To further penguin conservation, Boersma has put her political skills, learned in college when she was active in student government and in graduate school when she served on President Nixon's task force for Women's Rights and Responsibilities, to use by serving environmental interests around the world. She is a founder of the Global Penguin Society, has been an advisor to the United States Delegation to the United Nations World Population Conference in Romania, was an advisor to Disney's Animal Kingdom, and is on the board of the Peregrine Fund. Currently she heads the Center for Penguins as Ocean Sentinels at the University of Washington and is the co-chair of the International Union for the Conservation of Nature Penguin Specialist Group. She co-edited the book *Penguins: Natural History and Conservation* (2013), which was a University of Washington best seller and the top book published in Argentina in 2015 (*Pinguinos: Historia Natural y Conservacion*).

Although Boersma has won numerous conservation awards, the one she is most proud of is the Heinz Award in the Environment in 2009. (The Heinz Award in the Environment, established in 1993 by Theresa Heinz in memory of her late husband, US Senator John Heinz, honors individuals who have confronted environmental concerns with a spirit of innovation and who demonstrate the same blend of action and creativity in approaching the protection of our environment.) "Going to lunch with John Kerry and his wife, Theresa Heinz, in their house in Washington and having a ceremony in the portrait gallery was an amazing experience that I will cherish," she says. More than any accolade, though, what she is proudest of is detailing the natural history of Galápagos and Magellanic penguins. "What our studies show is that penguins are not that different than people. They're trying to make a living, raise a family, and be successful. Isn't that what most people try to do?"

Besides being an environmental advocate and a penguin researcher, Boersma is an educator. She has educated future conservationists for over four decades. One thing she tells her students is that it doesn't take a lot make a contribution. She uses Thoreau as an example. "If you go back to Walden Pond, he kept records of the phenology of those plants. People are using that data from the 1850s to see that plants are blooming earlier due to climate change. I'm sure he had no idea that data would be used to assess climate change." She worries that people have shorter attention spans nowadays, but she says, "Keeping detailed natural history notes and observations are incredibly important in informing us about the natural world."

If her biggest pride has been detailing the natural history of penguins, her most rewarding moments have also been with penguins, specifically with Turbo. "I check him several times a day when I'm in Punta Tombo because I like him," she says, recounting a story from the spring of 2016. "When I went to his nest he came out and greeted me, and then he started walking away. I said 'I bet you're going to the sea, and I'm going to follow along with you.' So I walked with him. We walked all the way to the sea, about three-quarters of a mile away. I said to him, 'When you go into the water, I'm not going in with you. I'm not going to get my feet wet! I'm just walking you that far.' We got down to the beach where the waves were coming in and he stopped, so I stopped. Then he continued over the wet rocks and headed to the water. After about ten meters, he stopped and looked at me, like 'aren't you coming?' And then off he went. He was gone for about ten days foraging."

With connections like this to wildlife and nature, Boersma worries about the state of the planet. "There are 7.2 billion people in the world. We are extremely out of balance with the natural world," she says. "And nobody's talking about the elephant in the room like we did even several decades ago, the need to control human numbers and consumption. Humans have to be smart enough soon to realize we have to do something about our consumption and our numbers. We each need to wrestle with the choices we make."

In terms of her own choices, she says, "I purposely did not have a child. I couldn't have done this work if I had children." But, she adds, "I feel like I have plenty of children. Not only do I have penguins, but I have had many graduate students in Argentina and the United States over the years." Another choice she has made is to spend several months each year away from home. "Being a field biologist is difficult because it's disruptive to friends and family," she says. "But I have a wonderful partner who works on whales, and she spends lots of time gone, too. People have to find their passion. Penguins are my passion. You can have an interesting life, but you have to pay attention to what you really want to do. I like the places where I work and the wildlife, and I have never been willing to give it up."

And she can't give up—Turbo is depending on her.

For more information on Dee Boersma, please visit www.penguinstudies.org and www.igalapagos.org.

CHAPTER 20

• • •

Mike Chase, PhD: Census Taker of African Elephants

"Elephants are Africa's proudest emblems. Africa without African elephants would have lost its soul."

—Mike Chase

Credit: Kelly Lander, Elephants Without Borders

Mike Chase.

W HEN MIKE CHASE, A FIFTH-GENERATION *Motswana* (an inhabitant of Botswana), was a child, his grandfather pulled him aside and said, "When you see an elephant, have a good look, because at the rate we're killing them, they might not be around when you're older."

Chase never forgot those words. Fast forward to 2016 and Chase is at the end of the Great Elephant Census (for which he is the principal researcher and leader), the first standardized, aerial survey of Africa's savanna elephants—and the largest comprehensive animal survey in Africa's history. Chase is attempting to see if what his grandfather said was indeed prophetic. He wants to answer a question that much of the world wants answered: What is the future for African elephants?

🐾

Born in 1973, growing up in the wilds of Botswana influenced every aspect of Chase's character today. "This country was only founded in 1966, so it's very young, and when I was growing up, it was truly a wild environment: few roads, limited modern infrastructure, and a very small population," he says. Chase spent much of his childhood in the bush with his father on safaris, and his early memories include seeing dust clouds created by enormous herds of zebra and wildebeest on their long-distance migration across the Makgadikgadi Pans (one of the largest salt flats in the world located in the northeastern part of the country). As for elephants, they were everywhere, etched into his mind since he was a baby. The five thousand to twelve thousand-pound herbivores were such a part of Chase's normal childhood existence that he says, "Asking me about the first time I saw an elephant would be like asking someone from the US if they recall their first time seeing a dog." He goes on to reflect upon the way these gentle giants have come to define his life: "When people ask why I chose elephants, I say elephants chose me. They are truly charismatic. I am still as intrigued by them today as I was as a child. I'm moved by their majesty, their intelligence, their historic struggle for survival."

Chase attended boarding school in South Africa and later completed his A levels in Zimbabwe. Chase was dyslexic and studying was difficult, but the challenge forced him to work harder and endure. When he graduated—doing so with high marks—he headed for the Okavango Delta (an approximately six thousand-square-mile oasis of inland delta in the Kalahari Desert of northern Botswana). He had read the diaries of early explorers' adventures to this region, saying that the Okavango Delta was one of the last truly wild places on earth. His mother was afraid that her son would disappear into the wilds and, realizing the passion and potential he had for conservation efforts, she sent an application on his behalf to the University of Natal in South Africa. Chase was accepted and he agreed to pursue his studies further. He obtained his master's degree and completed his thesis on the conservation of transboundary ecosystems in 1998.

Chase returned home to Botswana and worked for six years in the Okavango Delta with the nonprofit Conservation International (CI). While working to conserve the wildlife of the delta, he was chosen to do an aerial study of the region's elephants. "I was in complete awe when flying at a low level of three hundred feet over one of the most spectacular wilderness areas in Africa," says Chase. "It was breathtaking. I found it infectious. The survey enabled me to see clearly the country and the animals that roamed on it, and I realized that I had found my passion and possibly a means of contributing to conservation efforts in Botswana."

As he counted and tracked the magnificent herbivores from the air—flying over marshes and islands, floodplains and lagoons—Chase's mind filled with questions: Where were the elephants coming from? Were they in the delta year-round? Did they move with the seasons? What impact did they have on their environment? "As an ecologist I was intrigued by the numbers of elephants and that there was very little information on their ecology in Botswana, which happens to be one of their strongholds," he says. So little was known about such a large creature, yet without the knowledge of their habitat and their range, how could they be conserved? These thoughts sparked Chase's dream to survey the continent's elephants. But it would be some time before he realized that dream.

🐾

While working for CI, Chase met professor Curt Griffin from University of Massachusetts, Amherst—who at the time was a consultant for the organization. While flying surveys together, Griffin suggested that Chase apply for a scholarship for his PhD at the same institution. Griffin submitted a recommendation, and in 2001 Chase was accepted with a scholarship and traveled to the United States for the first time to begin studying for his doctorate. He spent the next six years travelling back and forth between Massachusetts and the Okavango, where he deployed satellite collars on elephants in order to track their movements.

The results of Chase's research shattered old assumptions about elephant movements, in particular the idea that they stayed mostly in one general area. Not only did Chase discover that they didn't stay in one area, but he documented what turned out to be one of the largest and longest migrations on the African continent. Elephants, Chase realized, could no longer be studied in isolation, one country at a time. "Elephants were telling us where they needed to go and what territory needed to be protected if they were to flourish," he says. "My findings were used to outline the boundaries of the newly organized Kavango-Zambezi Transfrontier Conservation Area (KAZA). Five neighboring countries—Botswana, Namibia, Zambia, Zimbabwe, and Angola—officially acknowledged that wildlife conservation transcended national boundaries."

Chase's thesis study was also the first to record what was happening with elephants in Angola. Before the nearly thirty-year civil war that lasted from 1975 to 2002, Angola was thought to have 200 thousand elephants. Although it was widely known that elephants were being slaughtered for their ivory to fund the war, nobody knew exactly what that slaughter looked like. Nobody even knew if there were any elephants left in the country. "In 2003, our survey revealed the elephant population to be about 350 in Angola," he says. At the same time, Chase found that those Angolan elephants that had not been killed had become "political refugees" in Botswana, seeking safety and sanctuary in a place renowned for its wildlife protection programs. Now that the war was over, Chase and his colleagues discovered that these elephants were moving out of Botswana, through Namibia, and repopulating southeast Angola. They were returning to their ancestral homelands. He hoped that would mean a flourishing population in the near future.

🐾

In 2004, while in the midst of earning his PhD (in 2007, Chase became the first *Motswana* to earn a doctorate in elephant ecology), he, together with his partner Kelly Landen, founded the nonprofit conservation trust Elephants Without Borders (EWB), which he took from the name of his thesis, in order to conserve what he calls "nature's great masterpiece." With an estimated 150 thousand elephants living in the northern region of Botswana (the largest elephant population remaining in Africa) and migrating between western Zimbabwe, Namibia's Caprivi Strip (a 280-mile protrusion of land between Botswana, Zambia, and Angola), southeast Angola, and southwest Zambia, EWB strives to identify wildlife migratory corridors, secure wild habitats, and elevate conservation of all wildlife.

"Our objective at Elephants Without Borders has always been to provide and support policy-making with science," explains Chase. "Our work remains grounded in data, and it's data that gives us a chance of saving Africa's elephants." It's not only elephants that Chase and his colleagues are trying to conserve. Their efforts have extended to include other species under their "umbrella"—an umbrella species being one with a large home range over vast habitat types, so that if their requirements are met, then the requirements of other species will be met as well. With this concept in mind, Chase says, "The fight to save the elephants is, in effect, a fight to save an entire ecosystem. At Elephants Without Borders, we believe that conserving the African elephant is the best way to try and secure conservation lands for the benefit of Africa's people and all of its wildlife."

Despite such important work, securing funding for EWB was not an easy task, and in 2007, Chase almost had to shut its doors. "I was about to give up on my dreams when the San Diego Zoo told me I was their new Henderson Endowed Post-Doctoral Research Fellow, a position which secured a salary and seed funding for five years." With the new funding, Chase was able to once again dream big.

Although Chase loves sitting in a plane, far from his problems on the ground, and refers to his flying time as "air therapy," the bureaucracy frustrated him. Dealing with political boundaries, one nation at a time, while trying to save an animal that spans borders grew frustrating. "Fragmented" is the word he uses to describe this work. He wanted to get a picture of elephants across the whole continent. "But that was just talk," he says. He knew that a pan-African census would be exorbitantly expensive and unthinkably labor-intensive. Twenty or more countries, each with its own agenda, would have to sign on. "The Great Elephant Census (GEC) was a pipedream," he says, "but I could never quite let it go."

In 2014, philanthropist Paul G. Allen and his sister Jody, who both share Chase's passion for elephants, contacted EWB and asked Chase if they could spend a day flying with him. After spending the day in the field collaring elephants together and getting to know each other, Allen asked Chase how he could "move the needle" on elephant conservation. "I suggested the GEC," says Chase. "Within a day, the Allens supported it. I said it would take five years and he said elephants don't have the luxury of that length of time. He suggested a two-year time frame. I expressed concern that it would double the original budget, but considering the urgency, Mr. Allen decided on the two-year census period. Within a week, the funds had been made available, and so began the launch of the greatest and most accurate animal count ever undertaken on the African continent." Chase was able to start his pipedream, an attempt to reliably estimate the numbers of elephants in Africa.

Before European colonization, Africa may have had over twenty million elephants; as recently as the 1970s, there were one million. In 2016, after completing the GEC, Chase and his colleagues estimated that there were 352,271 remaining savanna elephants in eighteen countries with Botswana holding 37 percent of this total, Zimbabwe 23 percent, and Tanzania 12 percent (with a loss of 60 percent of its elephants between 2009 and 2015). They found out that elephant populations in survey areas with historical data had decreased by an estimated 144,000 from 2007 to 2014, and populations were currently shrinking by 8 percent per year throughout the continent, primarily due to poaching, but also because of human-elephant conflict, habitat loss and fragmentation, and isolation of populations.

One result for Chase was particularly distressing—the low population of elephants in Angola—the site of his 2003 survey. He had hoped that with the movement of elephants back into Angola and the work of EWB to help facilitate that movement, he would find a thriving population. What he found was a huge disappointment. Chase explains:

> In 2014 we estimated there were 3,500 elephants in Angola, showing that they had indeed moved back, but there should have been many more considering the rate of immigration occurring during the early 2000s. What we realized was that the numbers were not as large as we expected because Angola has the highest poaching rate on the continent. As fast as

elephants move out of Botswana and back into Angola, they have been met with the poacher's gun and are running back to the safety of Botswana. Not many people know that Angola has the highest rate of elephant poaching in Africa. East Africa is mostly in the news, but the poachers have moved from East and Central Africa to Southern Africa. We just don't make the news as much as East Africa, even though the crisis here is just as bad. Angola is losing 10 percent of its elephants each year, a higher mortality rate than any other country surveyed in the GEC.

After he finished flying for the Great Elephant Census, many people asked Chase whether he was optimistic about the future of elephants. "My answer is always the same: if you look at the science about what's happening on earth and to elephants and aren't pessimistic, you don't understand the data," he says and adds, "but I'm a stubborn optimist. I don't want to spend my life sharing depressing statistics and fighting a losing battle for elephants. On days when I meet the people who are working to restore this earth and save elephants, I am optimistic."

It is not always easy, however, to stay positive when the obstacles to saving African elephants are so enormous, and at times Chase's stubborn optimism falters. "Wild things in Africa are under threat as never before," he says, citing exploding human populations as one of the major reasons for the threat. According to the Population Reference Bureau, over the next half century the population of Africa is projected to more than double—from 1.1 billion people to at least 2.4 billion—with nearly all the growth occurring in sub-Saharan Africa. Besides population growth, other threats to African wildlife include demand for wild meat, overhunting, habitat loss, animals living outside of protected areas, and lack of finances and governmental planning. "Many fear that the continent's most iconic animals may soon vanish from their natural habitat. The disappearance of lions, elephants, and others would mean the crumbling of vital ecosystems—and the loss of billions of dollars in tourism revenue—natural treasures provide a source of sustainable income to Botswana's people."

With these threats in mind, Chase plans to turn to education in his home country. "I've decided that a major share of all future funding for EWB will be spent on educating our children about the importance of conserving Botswana's natural heritage, which is still a custodian to almost 40 percent of Africa's elephants. And if we can in some small measure protect and look after this almost 40 percent, I think that's a vital conservation ambition."

While Chase reflects on the importance of education, he also thinks about what immediate actions need to happen in order to secure a future for elephants. Poaching has become synonymous in many people's minds with the decline of African elephants, but Chase has a different view of the poaching crisis. "There is hope to stop poaching," he says. "It is something that can be accomplished. The poaching crisis and the Great Elephant Census results have brought international attention to the plight of the elephants and to illegal wildlife trafficking and now is stimulating important changes that otherwise may have been left unnoticed or stayed stagnant." Chase believes that the more difficult task is ensuring safe, secure resources and space for wildlife to flourish. "Even if, or should I say, when, we cap the poaching crisis, we will still need to face this much larger contentious issue," he says.

Combatting such large problems can be depressing, yet Chase has a staunch belief in the work he and others are doing to save African elephants. "How do you measure 'success' when your study species is facing one of its bleakest moments in its natural history?" he wonders. "Yes, we are facing a dark time in elephant conservation, but let me assure you, Africa will always have elephants. Of that I am certain. Why? Because of the commitment of my country, Botswana, and its leadership under President Ian Khama and his brother Tshekedi Khama, the country's Environment, Wildlife and Tourism Minister, and other like-minded governments that are trying their best to conserve elephants and their habitats."

Elephants are not just a part of Chase's life; they are his life. "In one way or another, my life with elephants is the only career I ever imagined having. I work because I want to and not because I have to. It's part of my identity, and I love it." As such, he says that any sacrifices he does make, he makes willingly. "Sacrifices are amply compensated by the satisfaction I take from my work and my interactions with my colleagues and with the elephants." And he has had many memorable interactions with elephants, starting when he was nine years old and fell asleep in a car, only to be awoken to the car being shaken by an enormous bull elephant that then settled in next to him for a rest. But the most enjoyment he has had was nursing Naledi, a one-month-old orphaned elephant, back to health. "When she was fighting for her life, I was depressed, anxious, and worried. I felt the burden of her battle for survival resonated with our efforts to save elephants in the wild and that, in some small way, if I failed her, I would fail in my task to help her wild cousins. It was one of my proudest moments when I saw that she was recovering and out of the critical stage."

There was also an instance in 2011 when Chase was asked to help monitor a large female elephant, Gika, and her eight-year-old calf, Naya, who were both being released into Chase's beloved Okavango Delta. (Gika had been orphaned during a 1988 culling operation in South Africa, then had been sold to a circus, and had eventually come to live at a camp in the Okavango Delta.) Chase's role in the project was to camp out in a large enclosure built for Gika and Naya while they were getting used to being out alone in the wild. Once the pair became comfortable and used to their confines, the gate was opened. Within five days of their reintroduction, Gika and Naya joined up with previously released Nandipa and her wild calves, making the herd into a family of five. On August 22, 2013, while following the herd to collect dung samples, Chase and colleagues found out that Gika had given birth to her first calf in the wild. And, in December 2015, the group again was spotted, but this time with a calf following Naya's heels.

In summer 2016, Chase got a chance to see the elephants again when the entire herd came into the EWB research station. "During the day they were at the research station eating jackalberries," he says. "That night we were sleeping in our tent when we woke to see their shadows walking by in line, one behind the other, literally brushing the tarp, and low rumbling as they went. I wish I knew what they were saying!" He describes the story of the traumatized orphaned elephant and her calf being reunited with their wild cousins as a born free success story and a hallmark moment in his career. "There is nothing more magical than being among a family herd of elephants. They have a spiritual energy. Their enormity and strength can be very intimidating, but they are gentle, humble, majestic, compassionate, and intelligent, and I experience great enjoyment and peace when I am in their presence."

Elephants, a species that regularly draw global media attention, are often sponsored by celebrities across the world, and are like no other animal on the planet, have come to embody the fight for conservation.

Chase believes that empirically there is more reason for pessimism than hope. As the stubborn optimist, though, he knows that pessimism is not the answer. "We must focus on conservation success," he says. "If we do not find reason for hope, motivation will falter, and so will conservation action. How can we call the next generation of conservationists to action in an atmosphere of defeat? Telling people how bad things are clearly hasn't helped elephants. We must now attempt to give people a different message."

The message is this: we must break down barriers and come together instead of being driven apart. Saving the African elephant requires cooperation, not just from the five trans-boundary nations across which the great migration of the largest contiguous African elephant population occurs, but from the conservation community across the globe. Like Mike Chase, we must all be stubborn optimists.

African elephants need us.

For more information on Mike Chase, please visit www.elephantswithoutborders.org.

Acknowledgments

Lori and Janie would like to thank all the conservationists in this book for taking time from their ridiculously busy schedules, often coming out of remote locations, to make themselves available for interviews and editing chapters for accuracy. They would also like to thank Veronica Alvarado, their editor, and all the people at Skyhorse Publishing who believed in this book, and Carl Safina for his brilliant foreword. They each are grateful for the serendipitous ways of the Universe for bringing them together to dream this book larger than either of them would have done on their own. It has been a perfect collaboration.

Lori would like to thank her dear friends Suzette Curtis and Josee Scanlan for their encouragement, and Rachael Harris for her insistence that this book be traditionally published.

Janie would like to thank her family for their support, patience, love, and encouragement. She would also like to thank her writer's group who have spent Friday afternoons together for the past two decades.